THE CASE FOR
RIGHT-TO-WORK LAWS

The Case for Right-to-Work Laws

A Defense of Voluntary Unionism

BY

REV. EDWARD A. KELLER, C.S.C.

University of Notre Dame
Notre Dame, Indiana

The Heritage Foundation, Inc.
75 East Wacker Drive
Chicago 1, Illinois

Introduction

The mere mention of "Right-to-Work" laws causes an immediate and intense emotional reaction; one author comments:

> ". . . the compulsory union membership issue continues to be a focal point of acrimonious debate—at the collective bargaining table, on the picket line, in Federal and state legislative halls, before Federal and state administrative agencies, in the courts, and among all citizens concerned with grave matters of public interest. It raises in the minds of its proponents questions of economic right, of justice, of morality, and of principle."[1]

What basically is the issue involved in "Right-to-Work" laws that should produce such an effect? It is compulsory unionism *vs* voluntary unionism, that and nothing more. "Right-to-Work" laws seek to protect the right of the worker to join or not to join a union by making illegal, as a condition of employment, membership or nonmembership in a union.

Unfortunately, most of the debate has not been concentrated on this basic issue but has degenerated into accusation of bad motivation and sloganizing which have not served the cause of truth and charity.

This type of argument begins with the very designation "Right-to-Work." Opponents maintain the phrase is a sham and semantic nonsense because such laws do not give, create or guarantee a job. The implied accusation of dishonesty is not justified because the phrase "Right-to-Work" is a legal term of long standing, both here and in Free Europe.

Thus the Supreme Court after the Civil War, defined

[1]"Collective Bargaining," by Selwyn H. Torff, p. 75.

5

the "Right-to-Work" in decisions invalidating legislation which denied the right to engage in their professions to those who had supported the Confederate cause during the Civil War. More recently, after World War II, the Right-to-Work was used against a California law which denied Japanese fishermen their Right-to-Work at their occupation of fishing off the Pacific Coast.

> "It requires no argument to show that the *right to work for a living in the common occupations of the community* is of the very essence of the personal freedom and opportunity that it was the purpose of the Amendment [Fourteenth] to secure." [Emphasis added.]

Forty years ago (1915) Justice Hughes declared in *Truax* v. *Raich*, 239 U.S. 33:

In France as early as 1791 the Right-to-Work was proclaimed by law. Practically every country of Western Europe has used the term "Right-to-Work" as a legal phrase which connotes the Right-to-Work without undue encumbrance.

The accusation of dishonest sloganizing is unjustified therefore because it was natural that the legislators who enacted "Right-to-Work" laws would employ a legal term of such widespread and long-standing use.

It should be pointed out that the phrase "Right-to-Work" in the United States (or for that matter in Free Europe) is not a "Collectivist" right in the sense that the State has an obligation of guaranteeing work or a job to any and every worker. Right-to-Work in the American sense means that any worker, having the necessary qualifications, has the opportunity to seek work for whom he wishes, where he wishes and without undue interference. Because normally, a job is necessary for livelihood and therefore necessary for life itself, right to work is simply the extension of the inalienable right to life as announced in the Declaration of Independence.

In 1954 Justice Douglas in *Barsky* v. *Board of Regents*, 347 U.S. 442, 472, clearly defined the right to work:

"The right to work, I had assumed, was the most precious liberty that man possesses. Man has indeed as much right to work as he has to live, to be free, to own property. The American ideal was stated by Emerson in his essay on Politics, 'A man has a right to be employed, to be trusted, to be loved, to be revered.' It does many men little good to stay alive and free and propertied if they cannot work. To work means to eat. It also means to live. For many it would be better to work in jail, than to sit idle on the curb."

"Right-to-Work" laws, therefore, do not pretend to create work or give a right to an actual job; these laws seek merely to protect the constitutional and natural right to work from the restriction of compulsory union membership, which restricts the exercise of the right to work only to members of a union.

Purpose of Article

The purpose of this article is not primarily to express support for such laws, but to analyze the reasons underlying "Right-to-Work" laws. We hope to shed further light on this controversial topic, and thereby to be of assistance in furthering truth and justice and not merely a partisan point of view. Certain arguments and facts will be presented on the subject that have not been treated or at least have not been given sufficient emphasis.

Rev. John E. Coogan, S.J., Detroit University, stresses the need for a balanced approach to this controversial subject. He states:[1]

"There are many friends of the laboring man who feel that the priest-spokesmen for the union shop have left unspoken many of the things that demanded saying in explanation of its present outlawing by eighteen States of the Union.

[1]"Can Nothing Be Said for State 'Right-to-Work' Laws?" by John E. Coogan, S.J., *American Ecclesiastical Review*, Dec. 1955, p. 370.

Those spokesmen have not of course denied all union prov-
ocation for such laws. But their reference to such provoca-
tion is commonly so glancing and so sidelong that it might
almost as well have been omitted altogether. No matter
what the labor dispute, such champions of the union shop
as a rule find that the union is substantially in the right.
Such championing often seems with little regard for the
rights of the individual workman and of the eighteen outlawing States."

Msgr. George G. Higgins (Director, Social Action Department, N.C.W.C.), in his October 3rd, 1955, "Yardstick"
also agrees on the need for "a fair and objective study of
both sides of debatable issues" when he commented:

"The lead editorial in the September issue of The Sign
magazine, 'The Ethics of Controversy,' is required reading
for all of us who do any writing or public speaking on the
application of Catholic principles in the temporal order.
We recommend it very highly.

"The editors of The Sign are not surprised, or scandalized,
that there are sharp differences of opinion among American
Catholics; or that these differences sometimes result in pro-
longed public controversy. They regard this as normal, if
not inevitable.

"THREE SIMPLE RULES

"But their own correspondence, among other things, has
convinced them that the tone of Catholic controversy in
the United States is deteriorating rather rapidly. In their
opinion, we need a new approach—one that would 'raise
the level of American Catholic controversy to the standards
which generally prevail in older countries.'

"This new approach to the art of controversy would be
based on three simple rules: 1) an open-minded study of
Catholic social teaching in its entirety; 2) a fair and objective study of both sides of debatable issues, and 3) a
greater measure of fraternal charity which would impel all
of us to respect the integrity and good faith of those who

disagree with us, unless we have conclusive proof to the contrary.

"The last of these three rules would seem to be the most important at the present time. Surely we need more knowledge of principles and problems, more scientific research, both doctrinal and factual, but more than anything else we need a spirit of fraternal and/or a better sense of humor."

In the light of Msgr. Higgins' statement all concerned with the controversy on "Right-to-Work" laws should be willing to consider all the facts and arguments in support of "Right-to-Work" laws as well as to consider the facts and arguments that militate against such laws, for it is rare indeed that justice and truth are completely on one side in difficult matters of this kind. Unfortunately accusations of pro-labor or anti-labor bias have been injected into the controversy making difficult an objective appraisal of the issues involved.

Bishop Robert J. Dwyer of Reno, Nevada, made a pertinent observation in this regard when he stated:

"The Catholic Church is for Labor. . . . Her role in the emancipation of Labor and in the gradual building up its Christian rationale, in the recognition of its rights, privileges, and duties, has been decisive . . . But the Church is not for Labor to the exclusion of all other claims of rights and justice . . . The Church, however, has never made the fatal error of conceiving that Labor and its problems are her sole concern, or that other elements of the social structures should be ignored and forgotten. The role of the Church in human society is to maintain balance. The tendency of all partisanship is to upset balance.

"The point is important. There are many today, and among them not a few Catholic zealots, who would like to see the Church divorced from all other interests and married exclusively to Labor. They would have her throw her balance overboard and concern herself solely with Labor and its problems in a frankly partisan sense. They would have her declare for Labor simply because it is Labor, in total disregard for rights and justice. They seem to think that the Church should divest herself of judgment and common sense in any question involving labor. . . ." ("Sage and Sand," in *Nevada Register*, Oct. 15, 1954)

Archbishop Patrick A. O'Boyle, Episcopal Chairman of the Social Action Department of N.C.W.C. on October 18, 1955 commented:

"The Church is admittedly in favor of the organization of workers into unions for their own economic and moral betterment. But she is not pro-Labor in the sense of rationalizing or condoning or winking at labor's defects, nor is she pro-Labor in the sense of being anti-management or anti-anything else." (*The Tidings*—Los Angeles Diocesan paper—Oct. 21, 1955)

Legal Aspects of Voluntary Unionism

Because this problem is so enmeshed with the law, the legal aspects of the question must be explained. To bring the problem sharply into focus pertinent sections of the Utah "Right-to-Work" law, as passed in 1955, may be considered.

Its purpose, as declared in Section 1, is "To protect the right to work and to declare the public policy of the State of Utah with respect to membership or non membership in labor unions, labor organizations or any other type of associations as affecting the right to work. . . ."

Thereafter the Act goes on to provide:

> "Section 8. No employer shall require any person to become or remain a member of any labor union, labor organization or any other type of association as a condition of employment or continuation of employment by such employers.

> "Section 9. No employer shall require any person to abstain or refrain from membership in any labor union, labor organization or any other type of association as a condition of employment or continuation of employment."

See Appendix A for the complete text of a Right-to-Work Law—North Carolina. Both the North Carolina Supreme Court and The Supreme Court of the United States upheld the constitutionality of the North Carolina Right-to-Work Law.

Eighteen states:

Alabama, 1953	Georgia, 1947
Arkansas, 1947	Iowa, 1947
Arizona, 1947	Louisiana, 1954
Florida, 1944	Mississippi, 1954

Nebraska, 1947	South Dakota, 1947
Nevada, 1952	Tennessee, 1947
North Carolina, 1947	Texas, 1947
North Dakota, 1947	Utah, 1955
South Carolina, 1954	Virginia, 1947

have "Right-to-Work" laws. Some of these laws were adopted by popular referendum; the others by legislative statutes and by amendments to state constitutions.

A number of states have adopted labor legislation which incorporates substantial parts of the federal Norris-LaGuardia Act, including a declaration of public policy which reads substantially as follows:

"Though he [the worker] should be free to decline to associate with his fellows, it is necessary that he have full freedom of association, self-organization and designation of representatives of his own choosing . . ."

This language sets forth a public policy in favor of granting the worker full freedom of choice *to join* or *not to join* a union.

The courts of some of these states have, under this declaration of public policy, issued injunctions against picketing to force an employer to accept union shop agreements, e.g. *Retail Clerks Union* v. *Roth*, 218 Ind. 275, 31 N.E. 2d 986 (1941); *Bartenders Union* v. *Clark Restaurants*, 122 Ind. App. 165, 102 N.E. 2d 220 (1951).

Other courts, however, have held that to attach such significance to this declaration of public policy is not justifiable, e.g. *Denver Local Union No. 13* v. *Perry Truck Lines*, 106 Colo. 25, 101 P. 2d 436 (1940).

Legal Guarantee of Right to Organize

In Section 6 of the Clayton Act of 1914, Congress provided:

> "That the labor of a human being is not a commodity or article of commerce. Nothing contained in the antitrust laws shall be construed to forbid the existence and operation of labor . . . organizations, instituted for the purposes of mutual help, . . . or to forbid or restrain individual members of such organizations from lawfully carrying out the legitimate objects thereof; nor shall such organizations, or the members thereof, be held or construed to be illegal combinations or conspiracies in restraint of trade, under the antitrust laws."

When it enacted the Railway Labor Act in 1926, Congress sought to implement by statute the right of workers to organize unions and bargain with their employers collectively. Section 2, Fourth, of that Act provided that:

> "Employees shall have the right to organize and bargain collectively through representatives of their own choosing. The majority of any craft or class of employees shall have the right to determine who shall be the representative of the craft or class for the purposes of this Act. No carrier, its officers or agents shall deny or in any way question the right of its employees to join, organize, or assist in organizing the labor organization of their choice, and it shall be unlawful for any carrier to interfere in any way with the organization of its employees."

The Railway Labor Act was amended in 1934 to prohibit compulsory unionism; and further amended in 1951 to permit union shop agreements.

This latter amendment was opposed by union leaders as well as by employers. Mr. John T. Corbett, Assistant Grand Chief Engineer and National Legislative Representative, Brotherhood of Locomotive Engineers, as a witness, May 4, 1950, in the hearings on the bill to authorize union shop agreements, noted that

". . . during the time that Warren S. Stone [Grand Chief Engineer of the Brotherhood 1903–1925] was the grand chief engineer he took the position that the Brotherhood of Locomotive Engineers was such an outstanding organization that men should seek its membership. He didn't want any compulsion; he didn't want any closed shop; he didn't want any union shop—and possibly that policy is being reflected in my statement today." *Hearings Before Subcommittee of Committee on Labor and Public Welfare on S. 3295,* Eighty-first Congress, Second Session (1950), 86.

Mr. Stone was also quoted by a railway witness as follows:

"I do not believe in forcing a man to join a union. If he wants to join, all right; but it is contrary to the principles of free government and the Constitution of the United States to try to make him join. We of the engineers work willingly side by side with other engineers every day who do not belong to our union though they enjoy without any objection on our part the advantages we have obtained. Some of them we would not have in the union; others we cannot get." *Hearings Before the Committee on Interstate and Foreign Commerce, on H. R. 7789,* Eighty-first Congress, Second Session (1950), 100.

In 1953, Guy L. Brown, successor to Mr. Warren Stone as Grand Chief of the Brotherhood of Locomotive Engineers, commented:

"We support it [the union shop] now only on individual roads where other unions have put it into effect. Engineers just simply resent being told they must join anything. We still think that labor in the long run has a good-enough product that you won't have to force men to join. We must go along on a 'union shop' in some instances where it is necessary because of the possible encroachment upon our membership by some other organization." (*U.S. News & World Report,* Dec. 11, 1953, p. 71.)

Freedom of Association Extended by NIRA

In 1933 the National Industrial Recovery Act, under Section 7(a), guaranteed:

"(1) That employees shall have the right to organize and bargain collectively through representatives of their own choosing, and shall be free from the interference, restraint, or coercion of employers of labor, or their agents, in the designation of such representatives in self-organization or in other concerted activities for the purpose of collective bargaining or other mutual aid or protection;

"(2) That no employee and no one seeking employment shall be required as a condition of employment to join any company union or to refrain from joining, organizing, or assisting a labor organization of his own choosing."

The NIRA was declared unconstitutional in 1935 and in the same year the Wagner Act incorporated the NIRA guarantee of legal right to organize and bargain collectively, free from interference from employers. Section 7 of the Wagner Act stated:

"Employees shall have the right to self-organization, to form, join or assist labor organizations, to bargain collectively through representatives of their own choosing, and to engage in concerted activities for the purpose of collective bargaining or other mutual aid or protection."

The Wagner Act said nothing about a right not to join a union. But the Taft-Hartley Act, passed in 1947, provides that every worker:

". . . shall also have the right to refrain from any or all such activities except to the extent that such right may be affected by an agreement requiring membership in a labor organization as a condition of employment as authorized in section 8(a) (3)."

By this addition the Taft-Hartley Act formally restored the legal right of voluntary unionism and outlawed compulsory unionism in the form of the "closed shop," which makes membership in a union a condition of employment at the time the worker is hired. Somewhat inconsistently, the Taft-Hartley Act, in Section 8(a) (3), permits compulsory unionism in the form of the "union shop" when a union is able by collective bargaining or by other means, such as a strike, to win a union shop agreement from the employer. Under a union shop, a worker is not forced to belong to a union when he is hired but must join the union (which has won bargaining rights) after a certain period of time, usually thirty days, as a condition of continued employment. In other words, the worker, under a union shop agreement is compelled to join the union after thirty days whether he desires to or not, or else lose his job. Under a union shop agreement the employer must discharge the worker if he loses his membership in the union.

However, to protect the worker from the loss of his job for capricious and arbitrary dismissal from his union, the employer can be forced to discharge a worker who loses his membership in a union, only when:

> ". . . that membership was denied or terminated for reasons other than the failure of the employee to tender the periodic dues and the initiation fees uniformly required as a condition of acquiring or retaining membership." Section 8(a) (3) (B).

And in Section 8(b) (2), the Taft-Hartley Act makes it an unfair labor practice for a union

> ". . . to cause or attempt to cause an employer . . . to discriminate against an employee to whom membership in such organization has been denied or terminated on some ground other than his failure to tender the periodic dues and the initiation fees uniformly required as a condition of acquiring or retaining membership."

Sections 8(a) (3) and 14(b) of Taft-Hartley Act

The Taft-Hartley Act in Section 8(a) (3), permitted a union shop under certain clearly defined specifications. This section reads as follows:

"8(a) It shall be an unfair labor practice for an employer—

. . .

"(3) By discrimination in regard to hire or tenure of employment or any term or condition of employment to encourage or discourage membership in any labor organization: Provided, That nothing in this sub-chapter, or in any other statute of the United States, shall preclude an employer from making an agreement with a labor organization (not established, maintained, or assisted by any action defined in this subsection as an unfair labor practice) to require as a condition of employment membership therein on or after the thirtieth day following the beginning of such employment or the effective date of such agreement, whichever is the later. . . ."

But the Taft-Hartley Act did not stop here. By Section 14(b), it expressly affirmed the right of the states to prohibit compulsory unionism—the language of that paragraph reading as follows:

"Nothing in this Act shall be construed as authorizing the execution or application of agreements requiring membership in a labor organization as a condition of employment in any state or territory in which such execution or application is prohibited by state or territorial law."

This latter provision, as it provides so plainly, leaves to the states the right to guarantee voluntary unionism if they wish. It removes all possibility of argument that state "Right-to-Work" laws unlawfully invade an area preempted by the federal government.

"Right-to-Work" Laws Permitted under Wagner Act

Section 14(b) of the Taft-Hartley Act has been the object of bitter attack by union leaders, an attack which is rather difficult to understand in view of the fact that the section actually adds nothing to the law as it stood under the Wagner Act. In *Algoma Plywood Co.* v. *Wisconsin Board,* 336 U.S. 301 (1949),[1] unions argued that Sections 8 (3) and 10(a) of the Wagner Act[2] preclude the states from imposing restrictions upon compulsory unionism. The Supreme Court rejected the argument and ruled that these sections of the Wagner Act permitted the states to declare invalid compulsory unionism agreements. All Section 14(b) does is state the same principle in language that could not possibly be misunderstood.

Court Tests of the Right to Work

The Supreme Court in 1939 upheld the constitutionality of "Right-to-Work" laws in *Lincoln Union* v. *Northwestern Co.,* 335 U.S. 525. In that case it stated:

"Under employment practices in the United States, employers have sometimes limited work opportunities to members of unions, sometimes to non-union members, and at other times have employed and kept their workers without regard to whether they were or were not members of a union. Employers are commanded to follow this latter employment practice in the States of North Carolina and Nebraska. A North Carolina statute and a Nebraska constitutional amendment provide that no person in those states shall be denied an opportunity to obtain or retain employment because he is or is not a member of a labor organization. To enforce this policy North Carolina and Nebraska employers are also forbidden to enter into con-

[1]See Appendix B for Supreme Court decision regarding "Right-to-Work" Laws under the Wagner Act.
[2]See Appendix C for Sections 8 (3) and 10(a) of the Wagner Act.

tracts or agreements obligating themselves to exclude persons from employment because they are or are not labor union members." 335 U.S. at 527–528.

The unions argued in the *Lincoln Union* case that state "Right-to-Work" laws are unconstitutional because they deprive union workers of their "right" to force non-members into the union or out of work. To this, the Supreme Court said:

> "We deem it unnecessary to elaborate the numerous reasons for our rejection of this contention of . . . [the unions]. Nor need we appraise or analyze with particularity the rather startling ideas suggested to support some of the premises on which Appellants' [the unions'] conclusions rest. There cannot be wrung from a constitutional right of workers to assemble to discuss improvement of their own working standards, a further constitutional right to drive from remunerative employment all other persons who will not or cannot participate in union assemblies. . . ." 335 U.S. at 531.

More recently, the Supreme Court of Nebraska, in *Hanson* v. *Union Pacific Railroad Co.*, 160 Neb. 669, 71 N.W. 2d 526 (1955), held unconstitutional the Railway Labor Act as amended in 1951 permitting the union shop. Justice Wenke in delivering the opinion of the Nebraska Supreme Court stated:

> "Appellees contend this amendment to the Railway Labor Act, together with the contracts it authorizes, compels railway employees to become members of an association (Labor organization) against their will and thus deprives them of freedoms guaranteed by the First Amendment to the Constitution of the United States. They claim the right of the freedom of association, the freedom to join or not to join, as a First Amendment freedom.

> "The First Amendment to the Constitution of the United States provides: 'Congress shall make no law respecting an establishment of religion, or prohibiting the free exercise

thereof; or abridging the freedom of speech, or of the press; or the right of the people peacably to assemble, and to petition the Government for a redress of grievances. . . .'

"We think the freedom of association, the freedom to join or not to join in association with others for whatever purposes such association is lawfully organized, is a freedom guaranteed by the First Amendment. We also think the right to work is one of the most precious liberties that man possesses. Man has as much right to work as he has to live, to be free, to own property, or to join a church of his own choice for without freedom to work the others would soon disappear. It is a fundamental human right which the due process clause of the Fifth Amendment protects from improper infringement by the federal government. To work for a living in the occupations available in a community is the very essence of personal freedom and opportunity that it was one of the purposes of these amendments to make secure. . . .

"These rights should only be susceptible of restriction to prevent grave and immediate danger to interests which the government is obligated to protect. *West Virginia State Board of Education* v. *Barnette, supra; Thomas* v. *Collins,* 323 U.S. 516, S.Ct. 315, 89 L.Ed. 430. . . .

"We find no condition to have existed at the time the amendment was adopted to authorize any restriction of these rights. Consequently we think Congress was without authority to impose upon employees of railroads in Nebraska, contrary to our Constitution and statutory provisions, the requirements that they must become members of a union representing their craft or class as a condition for their continued employment. It improperly burdens their right to work and infringes upon their freedoms. This is particularly true as to the latter because it is apparent that some of these labor organizations advocate political ideas, support political candidates, and advance national economic concepts which may or may not be of an employee's choice." 71 NW. 2d at 543–546.

This decision of the Nebraska Supreme Court is now before the United States Supreme Court. The Court has been asked to review another case involving substantially the same problem. It is *Hudson* v. *Atlantic Coast Line R. Co.*, 89 S.E. 2d 441 (1955), from the Supreme Court of North Carolina. In this latter case, the Supreme Court of North Carolina upheld the 1951 Amendment to the Railway Labor Act but did not pass upon the constitutional aspects of the union shop as the Nebraska Supreme Court had done. The North Carolina court said:

". . . [We] will not undertake to determine whether an Act of Congress is invalid because violative of the Constitution of the United States except on a ground definitely drawn into focus by plaintiff's pleadings. . . . We defer consideration of such matters [that union shop violates the fundamental right to work and freedom of association secured by the Constitution of the United States] until a specific situation is presented by allegation and evidence." 89 S.E. 2d at 453.

A suit has been instituted against General Motors and the CIO-UAW by a GM worker named Smith (in whose name a large number of GM workers are bringing the suit) who contends that his rights are violated by the union shop agreement entered into by the CIO-UAW and GM in June 1955; he further contends that this agreement violates the public policy of Indiana, which declares that workers have the freedom to join or not to join a union. A state trial court rejected his contention. This case is now on appeal. *Smith* v. *General Motors Corp.*, Appellate Court of Indiana, No. 18774.

There is another interesting case, *Otten* v. *Staten Island Rapid Transit Ry. Co.*, involving a "religious objector." Mr. Otten maintains compulsory unionism, in the form of the union shop, violates his constitutional rights of free association and freedom of religion by compelling him to join an association contrary to his religious belief. In his brief, he states his position to be:

"In 1938 to about 1940 I was a faithful member of local
Union 922, I.B.E.W. In 1940 I was out of the Railroad for
period of 70 days, I worked for the Board of Transportation, City of New York. I was reinstated on February 1st,
1941 as a Third Rail Maintainer losing my seniority but
retaining my position. In 1948 hearing the word of God I
was converted. I have given myself over to my Lord, my
Saviour, and on reading His word written in Bible I find
that to do the will of God I cannot link oneself with Trade
Union, or any Organization. I was a member of Junior
Order American Mechanics. At that time upon being converted I sent them letter requesting my resignation on
account of my Christian principles. I was also a member
of the Veterans Association of the Baltimore and Ohio
Railroad. I sent in letter requesting my resignation due
to Christian principles and it was graciously accepted.
Upon giving self to the Lord one cannot become a member of any Organization. I am not governed by men, I am
governed by God, and it is no closed book, and if you will
permit I will read—

"Second Corinthians—Chapter 6—Verse 14.

" 'Be not diversely yoked with unbelievers; for what participation is there between righteousness and lawlessness?
or what fellowship of light with darkness?'

"Therefore, according to the scriptures one feels that he
must do the will of God. As I stated before one cannot link
himself with unbelievers. In Union, or other Organizations,
there are many believers in the Lord Jesus, and many unbelievers, so if there are unbelievers we cannot link with
them. So, therefore, we must separate ourselves from all
Organizations. I ask you Mr. Doyle if you can graciously
exempt me from becoming a member of your Trade Union
on these grounds. We are not opposed to paying any
equivalent of dues to a Charitable Organization such as
the American Red Cross or a local Hospital, other than
Union purposes. . . ."

Two federal district courts and two courts of appeals
have ruled against Mr. Otten, but it is expected that he will

try to carry his case to the Supreme Court of the United States. Two other men, Wicks and Jensen, of the same religious society, "Plymouth Brethren IV," brought similar cases in the courts. The two cases have been consolidated and are on appeal. They may also reach the Supreme Court.

The reason these cases are important is that the individuals involved are opposed to being compelled to belong to a union because they sincerely believe that their freedom of conscience is violated by their being compelled to belong to a union.

The Morality of "Right-to-Work" Laws

"Right-to-Work" laws have been designated as immoral by some clergymen, both Catholic and non-Catholic. The A.F. of L.'s *The Machinist* carried articles by Rev. William J. Kelley, O.M.I. (a Catholic priest); Rev. Dr. Walter G. Muelder (a Protestant minister); and Rabbi Israel Goldstein (a Jewish rabbi) which attacked "Right-to-Work" laws on moral grounds. These three articles were widely circulated as a single pamphlet. Other Catholic priests, who have opposed "Right-to-Work" laws, have been careful not to designate these laws as immoral per se. Thus Father John S. Cronin, S.S.,[1] commented:

> "Q How would you classify a priest speaking on right-to-work law?
>
> "I would call that a good example of a tough problem. Moral principles are involved, such as labor's right to organize and the state's right to prevent injustice practiced by labor unions. But there are also matters of practical judgment of fact in applying moral principles. Here we run into real difficulties.
>
> "Q What are the difficulties?

[1] *The Sign*, Nov. 1955, p. 17.

"The heart of the matter is that it is not always easy to apply moral principles in concrete cases. In the present instance, much depends on the motive and effect of the law. If its purpose and effect are to prevent legitimate unions and to exploit workers, then it is clearly immoral. If it is designed to prevent union abuses without hurting proper union activity, then such a law may be justified."

Father Leo Brown, S.J., Director of the Institute of Social Order, St. Louis University, while opposing "Right-to-Work" laws in an article entitled "Right-to-Work Legislation" (Oct. 1955, *The Catholic Mind*, p. 606) stated:

". . . Nothing in this paper need be understood as implying that workmen are morally obliged to belong to labor unions. People can consistently advocate the legal liberty of a group of workmen to make union-shop contracts while defending their moral liberty to decide not to enter into such contracts or even to decide not to form a union."

The opposition to "Right-to-Work" laws in the Catholic Press has been so strong that the impression is given that such legislation should be condemned on moral grounds and/or as contrary to fundamental social doctrine. In fact, the opposition in the Catholic Press has been so one-sided as to create the impression that there is only one side to this controversial issue.

Regarding the divided opinion within the Catholic Church on such controversial issues as "Right-to-Work" laws Bishop Dwyer, Reno, Nevada, stated in his Nov. 12, 1954, *Sage and Sand* (the week after the Nevada "Right-to-Work" law had been upheld by popular referendum):

"Who is entitled to speak in the name of the Catholic Church? Whose word are we to trust as the expression of her mind? Few questions reflect a greater degree of confusion in the popular mind, whether asked by Catholics themselves or by those outside the Church. They are constantly recurring, in matters of general or particular interest, in matters transcending time and in the purely contemporary. Only recently they were raised here and elsewhere throughout the nation in connection with a moot point of labor legislation. Individual priests were widely quoted in support of one side of the issue, and the impression was fostered that their opinion necessarily represented the thinking of the Catholic Church. . . .

"Now it happens that the sphere of morals is less well defined than the sphere of faith. This is not to say that the Church is uncertain about what is moral or immoral. It is merely to point out that the problem of morality is inextricably interwoven with all human relations. It is bound up with government, with politics, with economics, with sociology, with art, with literature, with applied science, and even with entertainment. It involves the application of the virtues of justice, prudence, temperance, and fortitude to all these manifold and highly intricate relations. Where the distinction between right and wrong is clearly defined, the Church has not hesitated to speak out. Thus, in the political field she has condemned Socialism and Communism, and in the field of social behavior she has condemned birth prevention and mercy killing, not to speak of genocide. In the wake of the industrial revolution, she has given her closest attention to the vexed questions which have arisen in labor-management relations, attempting to define what is basic and minimal for the preservation of human rights and human dignity.

"But she has not pronounced, and she could not reasonably be expected to pronounce, on every item of particular legislation throughout the free world. Especially is this true in areas where debate is still justified. All such issues are by no means solidly black or white. It is not always clear whether they are injurious to human rights or are actually beneficial to them. In such areas she prudently prefers to abide the clarification of the points under debate. In other words, the Church is not a sort of universal umpire ready at all times to jump into every discussion with a cut-and-dried answer.

"In many instances individual theologians and even individual Bishops may feel that the issues are sufficiently clear to warrant their pronouncement upon them. The Church, save in notorious cases of imprudent action or obviously faulty thinking does not forbid this. Indeed, she is far more liberal in this regard than most of the professional liberals themselves. Her common sense and her long experience of human events have taught her that trial and error are the best solvents of many problems where rights and wrongs are not absolutely defined. Nor does she follow a policy of prohibiting discussion and debate, particularly among her qualified theologians. All she asks is that charity be preserved and that it be made clear that she has not officially spoken to end the matter.

"The difficulty is that some theologians and Catholic publicists are prone to write and speak as though they were the Holy Father himself. Instead of stating the facts and drawing their conclusions, with emphasis upon the actual limitations of their authority, they sometimes create the impression that they have a private pipeline to infallibility. It is unavoidable that a certain amount of confusion should arise from this.

"It is not the Church that is at fault, obviously, but the overzealous or overopinionated among her children. Nevertheless, it is a tribute to her basic tolerance that she prefers to encounter this risk rather than to stifle intelligent discussion. . . ."

This rather lengthy quotation is given because it is such a clear statement and should dispel the confusion regarding the right of Catholics to favor or oppose such legislation as "Right-to-Work" laws, so long as the issue is debatable.

A question put to Father Cronin in *The Sign* magazine of November 1955 was this:

"Why do you hedge all your answers?"

He replied: "Because labor-management problems are usually too complex for easy 'yes or no' answers. I could think of situations which might justify strikes by government workers, jurisdictional or sympathy strikes, and even political strikes. Each case has to be judged on its own merits."

That the moral issues involved in such laws are debatable because they are far from clear, is attested to by Father Francis J. Connell, C.SS.R., Dean of the School of Sacred Theology of Catholic University, in the following statement:

"I have been asked several times to write about the 'right-to-work' laws but until now I have hesitated to comply, because I feel that my knowledge of labor conditions in this country is very meagre. However, I believe that I can at least expound the moral principles pertinent to the matter.

"In the June, 1947, *American Ecclesiastical Review* (pp. 429-30) I discussed the question whether or not a working man is bound in conscience to join a union. I stated that Msgr. John A. Ryan and Father Oberle (exponent of ACTU) favored the affirmative view, while the Irish writer, Dr. George Clune, defended the negative. I stated that I myself was inclined to the latter view, and that I did not care to charge a man with mortal sin if he did not care to join a union. At the same time I pointed out that if in particular circumstances the union needed the cooperation of all the workers in a particular field, there would be an obligation on all individual working men to join it.

"It is worthy of note that some of the Catholics who have condemned the 'right-to-work' laws in recent times have given the impression that theirs is the common teaching of Catholic theologians. I have not read any articles in which my view was cited or quoted.

"I still hold the view I expressed in 1947—that there is no Catholic principle to the effect that every worker is bound to join the union. Neither do I believe that there is any Catholic principle which condemns the 'right-to-work' laws. It is true, the Catholic Church upholds the principle (of natural law) that legislation that would unduly restrict the right of workers to form unions and to act through these organizations for their reasonable welfare or that would injure social and economic progress would be immoral. Those who believe that the laws in question would produce such evils have a perfect right to expound and to defend their views and to oppose such legislation. But I cannot see how they can propose their views as the teaching of the Catholic Church. They can propose them as *their own conclusions from a principle taught by the Catholic Church*. On the other hand, if other Catholics believe that the 'right-to-work' laws do not produce evil results but rather help to adjust industrial and economic conditions, they are fully free to uphold such legislation, *as their own view*, without denying or opposing any Catholic principle. As I said, I myself am not sufficiently familiar with all the industrial conditions to entitle me to favor definitely either side: but I do contend that what is involved is an application of principles, not principles themselves. As we all know, two intelligent and sincere persons can agree on a principle, and yet come to opposite conclusions in applying it to concrete cases.

"Hence, a Catholic lawyer would be allowed to work for an organization that favors the laws in question, unless he were aware that the organization has some immoral design, such as the destruction of unions or undue curtailment of the workers' rights. In such a case, he could not in conscience cooperate. But if a lawyer and the organization that hires him believe the 'right-to-work' laws will be helpful toward adjusting conditions for both employers and employees, and will serve as a protection against unreasonable claims by unions—and I believe that some are sincere in their belief that such will be the effect of such laws—they are fully within their rights if they promote such legislation. . . ."[1]

The Editor of *The Record* (Diocesan paper of the Archdiocese of Louisville, Ky.) in an editorial entitled

[1]Letter written by The Very Rev. Francis J. Connell, Dean of Sacred School of Theology, University of America, Washington, D.C., to The Very Rev. Msgr. Philip M. Hannan, J.C.D., Washington, D.C., May 31, 1955.

"Good Arguments Favor Right-to-Work Laws" (July 1, 1955) made some pertinent observations regarding the controversy:

GOOD ARGUMENTS FAVOR
RIGHT-TO-WORK LAWS

On page 2 we are happy to carry another letter from Joseph L. Lenihan[2] on the subject of right-to-work laws. We regard the letter as particularly fortunate for several reasons.

For one thing, refusing all recourse to slogans and snarl words it deals directly with the issues. Secondly, it is a good example of the way in which a Catholic layman may legitimately approach a controversy in which he finds "theologians" and "members of the hierarchy" lined up on the other side.

Although at first we could see nothing wrong with it, we have been forced to conclude that the term "immoral," as applied to the right-to-work laws, was most unfortunate.

WHEN IS A THING IMMORAL?

A thing is immoral if it is clearly opposed to the moral law. But how can the right-to-work laws be regarded as clearly opposed to the moral law when there are weighty arguments available to show that they are designed to protect human rights?

At least we ourselves are bound to admit that, in the limited manner in which the controversy has been carried on in this paper, the results are all in favor of those who support the right-to-work laws.

WHAT ABOUT THE "ARGUMENT
FROM AUTHORITY"

One more thing. What about the "argument from authority" in a matter of this kind, the argument that runs:

[2]Letter of Joseph Lenihan, in same paper, is quoted on page 73 of the text.

"Father X, eminent theologian, and X members of the hierarchy hold . . . "? Does such an argument carry ponderable weight?

In theology proper, the argument from authority is of the utmost significance. But in other fields it is often the weakest of all arguments. We do not see how the decision concerning right-to-work laws can be regarded, at the present stage of our knowledge, as a theological decision. Therefore, let the argument go on, peacably and reasonably, without any fear of running into a censure of the Church.

Incidentally, we should like to remind our readers once more of the availability of our "letters" page. If Catholic laymen in the past have not felt free to discuss in their diocesan newspaper the questions in which they were interested, this atitude should be corrected. Mr. Lenihan's letter is a fine example of the approach open to Catholic laymen who feel they have something to say on the questions of the day.

Bad Motivation

Generally the opposition to "Right-to-Work" laws can be summarized under four heads: Motivation, Union Security, "Free Rider" and Economic Progress and Freedom of Contract.

Some opponents of "Right-to-Work" laws base their opposition on implied immoral Motivation. In effect they argue that these laws are immoral because the proponents of such laws are accused of being motivated by a "union-busting" attitude or by a general anti-union antagonism. The following from a Catholic Social Action Bulletin, while rather strong in tone is quite typical:

"For the past few months, an insidious 'Right-to-Work' campaign has been going on in many states. This high sounding, but hypocritical movement has for its goal the destruction of labor unions. This goal, of course, is never openly stated. Under the guise of protecting the individual worker, an effort is being made to completely destroy his inherent rights . . . Without unions the profit of the Pharisee is guaranteed . . . The backers of this campaign are intent only on exploiting the worker. . . ." (*Social Action Bulletin* of the Archdiocesan Labor Institute, St. Louis, March, 1953.)

The "bad" motivation argument is a very weak argument; in fact it is no argument at all because it doesn't prove that "Right-to-Work" laws are moral or immoral. So long as such laws do not deny "the natural right to form associations" one cannot accuse sponsors of such laws of having as their "goal, the destruction of labor unions." Even if some of the sponsors of "Right-to-Work" laws (and I don't doubt that there are such sponsors) are motivated by an anti-union bias, that would not make laws, which permit voluntary unionism, immoral per se. Even the sponsoring by the communists of a morally good law would not make the law immoral. Those sponsors of "Right-to-Work" laws who are motivated by immoral motives may be guilty of sin, but their sin doesn't make the laws immoral.

Another argument that implicitly assumes improper motivation is that the strongest support for "Right-to-Work" laws comes from business associations. However, "Right-to-Work" laws, despite propaganda to the opposite, do not favor employers but favor individual employees by seeking to protect individual workers from compulsory domination by union leaders.

Moreover, even if an employer were motivated by an anti-union bias, he could not use "Right-to-Work" laws to "bust" unions. It should be pointed out that Arizona, Florida and Nebraska passed their "Right-to-Work" laws by Constitutional Amendment which required a popular vote. Nevada passed its "Right-to-Work" law by popular referendum and defeated by the same method an attempt to repeal it. This can be offered as an answer to the argument that only employer groups back "Right-to-Work" laws.

In refutation of the contention that all or most of the proponents of "Right-to-Work" laws are motivated by an anti-union, "labor exploiting" motive, one can quote from individuals who can be classified as pro-union and yet who opposed compulsory unionism. President Franklin D. Roosevelt said:

> "I tell you frankly that the Government of the United States will not order, nor will Congress pass legislation ordering, a so-called closed shop.

> "It is true that by agreement between employees and employers in many plants of various industries the closed shop is now in operation. This is a result of the legal collective bargaining, and not of Government compulsion on employers or employees. It it also true that 95 percent or more of the employees in these particular mines belong to the United Mine Workers Union.

> "The Government will never compel this 5 percent to join the union by a Government Decree. That would be too much like the Hitler methods toward labor." (*Collective Bargaining*, by Selwyn H. Torff, p. 76.)

Justice Brandeis, who was a great friend of labor, advised against the closed shop.

> "The objections, legal, economic and social," he said, "against the closed shop are so strong and the ideas of a closed shop so antagonistic to the American spirit that the insistence upon it has been a serious obstacle to union progress."

Donald R. Richberg, Co-author of the 1926 Railway Labor Act and of the National Industrial Recovery Act of 1933; General Counsel of NRA from 1933 to 1935 and Chairman of the N.R.A. Board in 1935, during the first Roosevelt Administration, stated:

"The entire value of labor organization to the workers lies in this power of the workers to control their representatives. The basis of that control and the only assurance that it will continue, is found in the right and freedom of the individual worker to refuse to support an organization or a representative whose judgment or good will he does not trust. But how can a man trust his servant who assumes to be his master and says: 'You must obey me, or I will cut your throat!' "

The Academy of Political Science conducted a symposium on "The Right-to-Work." Professor Neil W. Chamberlain of Yale University presented the arguments in favor of union security or compulsory unionism. Professor Chamberlain, however, made the following comment regarding motivation:

". . . First, it avoids any reliance on compulsory union membership, and thereby avoids the sacrifice of principle which I believe many people genuinely affirm. I know that unions have often held to the belief that such principle is only a convenient shield for economic interest, and that such principle will be readily enough sacrificed when it pays to do so. The unions may well be right in specific instances, but I feel sure that there are numbers of people who are sympathetic to unions who nevertheless oppose compulsory membership. Some, such as Justice Rand in Canada, have rejected it because it would deny to the individual 'the right to seek work and to work independently of personal association with any organized group.' This objection becomes increasingly relevant as unions, which are part of a larger labor movement, spread their activities into the broader arena of national politics, where their activities are less closely related if not sometimes actually unrelated to the business of providing representation in a specific bargaining relationship, and where individual employees for that reason may object to forced association.

"But I do not choose to argue here the right and wrong of such a position; I am merely stating my own belief that principle, however enlightened or misguided, plays a substantial part in arousing opposition to the union or closed shop, and the unions may as well recognize that fact. . . . The unions have said that among those opposed to the closed shop, principle is only a cloak for expediency. While I think they overstate their opposition, it may be worth meeting their argument by removing whatever cloak is there and exposing the real issue more sharply, free of the obscuring shadows of the issue of forced association through compulsory membership."[3]

While these quotations do not prove or disprove the morality of "Right-to-Work" laws they do prove that one cannot accuse all proponents of voluntary unionism of being guilty of anti-union bias and of immoral motivation. Many (including myself), favor our anti-trust laws and other laws restricting business. One cannot legitimately argue that those who, in principle, believe these laws to be necessary and good, are motivated by an anti-business or anti-management prejudice. Many businessmen and business associations have declared in favor of these anti-monopoly laws. Likewise the accusation of anti-union should not and cannot be made against those who believe, in principle, that compulsory unionism is unjustified under present conditions in the United States.

It is precisely here that objective analysis is most needed because the use of "smear" tactics by unjustified accusation of improper motivation merely stirs up emotions and prevents this problem from being studied and solved on the basis of objectivity rather than on imputed subjective motivation.

Union Security

The moral argument against "Right-to-Work" laws based upon union security is that such laws so weaken unions

[3]*Proceedings of the Academy of Political Science,* Vol. XXVI, May 1954, No. 1, pp. 12–13.

as to make the right of association ineffective. The argument implicitly, at least, maintains that union security is necessary for union survival and therefore "Right-to-Work" laws are immoral because they prevent workers from effectively exercising their natural right of free association.

Certainly closed and union shop agreements do give great security to unions; for this reason they are usually called by unions "union security clauses." Admitting this does not mean that voluntary unionism, as permitted by "Right-to-Work" laws, makes impossible effective union security. Whatever may have been the situation in former years, today there is no realistic ground upon which one could base the contention that "Right-to-Work" laws can destroy unions or prevent either their formation or their effective functioning.

An authority in the field of labor-management relations states:

> "If the union-survival theory were to be accepted as the motivating basis for the demand for compulsory union membership today, there would be little support in reality for such a demand. The American labor movement has not been feeble for a long time; it is vigorous, aggressive, and effective. It is protected by law and fortified by strength. It is one of the most dominating economic, political and social institutions in the nation. It is beyond the capability of employers to destroy it, even if they so desired or attempted. And the day of attempts by employers to destroy unions as such seems long past; 'union busting' exists today largely as a propaganda term. For the great majority of employers, labor unions and the collective bargaining process are established facts of economic life. Whatever the compulsory union membership issue may once have involved it is no longer an issue that involves the survival of labor unionism in the United States."[1]

The opponents of "Right-to-Work" laws who argue that these laws will destroy unions ignore the provision of the Taft-Hartley Act which guarantees the right of workers to

[1]*Collective Bargaining,* by Selwyn H. Torff, p. 75.

establish and to join unions without interference from their employers. It may be argued that the Taft-Hartley Act covers only interstate business and therefore does not protect the workers in intra-state business. This is not true because the "Right-to-Work" statutes also guarantee the right of workers to join or form labor unions. The Louisiana Law, for example, explicitly states:

"Section 1. Be it enacted by the Legislature of Louisiana, that it is hereby declared to be the public policy of Louisiana that the right of a person or persons to work shall not be abridged on account of membership or non-membership in any labor union or labor organization.

"Section 10. Nothing in this Act shall be construed to deny or abridge the right of employees by and through a labor organization or labor union to bargain collectively with their employer."

The Taft-Hartley Act does not give to the states the power to deny workers the right to join or form unions; it merely grants to the states the power to prohibit or regulate compulsory unionism. To argue otherwise is to distort the truth. Both Federal and state laws fully protect the right of workers to organize and bargain collectively without interference from their employers.

But, it might be argued where there is voluntary unionism, the union can be destroyed or weakened by favoritism of the employer toward non-union workers or discrimination against union members.

Those who so argue ignore Section 9(a) of the Wagner Act and of the Taft-Hartley Act which requires that:

"Representatives designated or selected for the purposes of collective bargaining by the majority of the employees in such unit for the purposes of collective bargaining in respect to rates of pay, wages, hours of employment or other conditions of employment."

This is called the principle of "exclusive representation" which requires that when the majority of employees in an appropriate bargaining unit (which may be a department, a whole plant or a group of plants) select a union as their bargaining agent, that union becomes the exclusive bargaining agent for all the employees in that unit, even though they are not all members of the union. This provision prevents individual bargaining by non-union workers and therefore fully protects union security against non-union minority bargaining.

Experience under Voluntary Unionism

The best answer to the arguments that union survival and union security are threatened under "Right-to-Work" laws is the actual experience under such laws. Unionism in the CIO, A.F. of L. and Independent Railway Unions made its greatest progress in the past fifteen years under voluntary unionism. The CIO-UAW only in June, 1955 won a union shop agreement from General Motors, which in effect, simply recognized an actual situation of almost 100 per cent unionization in GM plants under voluntary unionism. Experience under the Railway Labor Act, which from 1934 to 1951 prohibited the union shop, showed that union membership in the non-operating railway unions tripled during this period of voluntary unionism. What better showing could one ask that unions do not need compulsory membership to grow and function effectively?

In 1942 some of the railway unions demanded compulsory union membership. The resulting dispute was referred by President Roosevelt to the Sharfman Board which not only held that the demand could not be granted consistently with the law as it then stood but found that the arrangement was not necessary for the security of the unions. The Board said:

"Such an examination leaves the Board unconvinced on the ground of necessity. In the first place, the unions are not suffering from a falling off in members. On the contrary, as stated earlier; membership has been growing and at the present time appears to be the largest in railroad history, with less than 10 per cent nonmembership among the employees here represented.

"Second, the evidence presented with respect to danger from predatory rivals seemed to the Board lacking in sufficiency; especially so in the light of the evidence concerning membership growth.

"Third, no evidence was presented indicating that the unions stand in jeopardy by reason of carrier opposition. A few railroads were mentioned on which some of the unions do not represent a majority of their craft or class, and do not have bargaining relationships with the carrier. But the exhibits show that these unions are the chosen representatives of the employees on the overwhelming majority of the railroads, and that recognition of the unions is general. The Board does not find therefore that a sufficient case has been made for the necessity of additional protection of union status on the railroads." (Supplemental Report to the President by the Emergency Board, May 29, 1943.)

When the leaders of the same railroad unions went before Congress in their successful attempt to secure legislation legalizing the union shop, their chief spokesman frankly admitted that compulsory union membership was not necessary to strengthen the unions in their industry-wide bargaining. He said, "If I get a majority of employees to vote for my union as a bargaining agent, I have got as much economic power at that stage of the development as I will ever have." H.R. 7789, Eighty-first Congress, Second Session, May 9, 1950, pp. 20–21.

The experience of the sixteen states which had passed "Right-to-Work" laws prior to 1953 was surveyed by the Missouri State Chamber of Commerce. Mr. W. R. Brown, Director of Research, Missouri State Chamber of Commerce, in answer to the question "Do right-to-work laws destroy unions or hamper collective bargaining?" made this frank statement:

"It is impossible to obtain accurate figures on union membership by states; therefore, no categorical statement on over-all union growth in Right-to-work States can be made. However, letters from businessmen indicate that the Right-to-Work laws have not stopped union growth in their particular businesses. Also, studies by Prof. DeVyver of Duke University on Unions in the South indicates that most unions have continued to grow despite the Right-to-Work laws.

"It is, of course, probable that union growth might have been faster if it were not for the Right-to-Work laws because they require the union to sell the worker on the value of union membership instead of compelling the employer to force employees to join unions against their will.

"It is also conceivable, as Prof. DeVyver said in his 1948 study that the Right-to-work laws . . . 'may make it difficult for unions to retain their membership if wage increases are not periodically forthcoming . . . Today during prosperity and full employment membership increases, and round after round of wage increases keep the members active. When these rounds of raises stop, there is a real question whether union membership will decrease, particularly in light of the limitations to union security found in the Taft-Hartley Law and the state anti-closed shop laws. The answer to this problem will depend upon how well union leaders have convinced their members of the lasting benefits to workers of organization in an organized society and upon the amendments to the Taft-Hartley Law.'

"However, the prospect of some loss in membership with declining business conditions is not a problem that is peculiar to labor organizations—it is just as much of a problem, if not more, for business organizations."

More recent evidence is offered for Texas (one of the eighteen states with a "Right-to-Work" law enacted in 1947), by Frederic M. Meyers, Associate Professor of

Economics, University of Texas. Professor Meyers' testimony is particularly valuable because he testified as the expert economic witness for the defendant unions in the *Sandsberry* v. *IAM* case (Texas Court of Civil Appeals, Amarillo, 1954); he also was employed for a number of years by an economic bureau specializing in research for labor unions.

In a paper read at the 1954 Annual Convention of the Industrial Relations Association and titled "The Growth of Collective Bargaining in Texas—A Newly Industrialized Area," Professor Meyers states:

> "The first outstanding fact is that unionism in Texas has been growing extremely rapidly in the past twenty years. . . . The rate of unionization in Texas has probably, throughout the entire period under discussion, exceeded that of the rest of the country."

In a specific study of the effect of "Right-to-Work" laws, Professor Meyers in an article in the *Industrial and Labor Relations Review*, October, 1955, entitled "Effects of Right-to-Work Laws: A Study of the Texas Act" states:

> "It is virtually impossible to measure the precise effect of these laws on union organization, for no one can know what would have happened if another statutory environment had existed. However, the available evidence indicates that at least in manufacturing industry, the rate of growth in unionization in Texas has been very rapid since 1938 and has shown no significant diminution since 1947, when the law in question was passed (along with other highly restrictive labor legislation). Accompanying a great growth in industrialization and and employees, the proportion of manufacturing workers covered by collective agreements has grown from almost nothing in 1938 to about 50 per cent as of 1953. . . .

> "The tentative conclusion, then, is that if measured by the objectives of retarding unionization and destroying existing unions, the Texas 'right-to-work' law has not been very effective. . . .

"On the basis of limited evidence, it appears that legal restrictions on formal union security clauses in Texas have had little effect on the rate at which employees are initially organized, except in the construction industry, local trucking, the printing trades, and perhaps a few other cases where organizing the employer has been the traditional tactic. Even in these cases, restrictions on secondary pressures have probably been much more important than those on union security contracts. . . ."

Professor Meyers then gives the reason why unionism in the South was weak prior to World War II:

"The data, then, would suggest that the low rates of union incidence in Texas and the South have not, historically, been a result of mere location, but because the South and Texas have been preindustrial. They would suggest that as these areas become primarily industrial, they will become increasingly union. In a sense, the South represents a guarantee of continued growth of the American labor movement."[1]

This point is very important because it is an answer to the argument that "Right-to-Work" laws have been enacted in the South primarily because the South is anti-union. Unionism has been weak in the South because this region was dominantly agricultural. Unionism has made little headway in agriculture any place in the country.

Free Rider Argument

Another argument advanced to prove the immorality of "Right-to-Work" laws is that in permitting "open shops" the non-union worker receives the benefit of being represented by the union, without paying his share of the cost of operating the union. He is called a "free rider" by unions.

[1]"The Growth of Collective Bargaining in Texas" (1954 Annual Convention of The Industrial Relations Research Association), pp. 3–5.

Union leaders stress this argument of being forced to "service" non-union workers under the principle of "exclusive representation." What is not told is that "exclusive representation" was fought for strenuously by the unions on the ground that if they did not bargain for the non-union workers, the employer could use favoritism toward the non-union workers as a means of weakening or destroying the union. In all fairness, therefore, it should be pointed out that the non-union workers in an open shop today are not "free riders" but forced riders since under the Taft-Hartley Act they lose their right to bargain individually with their employers and are forced to bargain through the union.

Rev. Francis J. Connell, C.SS.R., Dean of the Sacred School of Theology, Catholic University, made a significant remark about the "free rider" argument when he stated:[1]

> "Let me add that we must be careful in our use of the argument that if a man gets the benefit of a union, he must join that union. I believe there is a flaw in this statement. It should be said, rather, that if a man benefits by a union he is bound to return some benefits to his fellow workers—but not necessarily by joining the union. He might do his share toward benefiting them by setting a high example of a conscientious diligent worker, or by visiting his fellow workers in their sickness or by working as a St. Vincent de Paul member for their benefit. The argument in question is likely to prove a boomerang for Catholics. It is the same argument that anti-Catholics use to make us pay taxes on our school and church property: 'If you get the benefit of fire protection, etc. for your property, you should pay for it.' We answer that we do make compensation to the state by the things of a spiritual value we provide for the public. I believe a similar response might be made by the man who does not join a union."

[1]Letter written to The Very Rev. Msgr. Philip M. Hannan, J.C.D., Washington, D.C., May 31, 1955, by The Very Rev. Francis J. Connell, C.SS.R., Dean of Sacred School of Theology, Catholic University of America, Washington, D.C.

At most one might argue that the non-union worker, when he is represented or "serviced" by the union under "exclusive representation" should pay his part of that cost in the form of initiation fees and normal dues. Whether this could ever be an obligation would depend upon circumstances such as, for example, a large labor turnover in small plants where the financial support of non-union workers would be necessary for the survival of the union. Even in this case, it would be difficult to prove with certainty that non-union workers would be morally obligated to pay dues.

Some argue that there is such an obligation because they attribute every economic gain of workers in modern times to unionism. This would be very difficult to prove. This argument ignores the tremendous increase in the standard of living of the ordinary workingman in the first thirty-five years of this century when unionism was relatively weak and practically limited to the craft unions.

On May 12 and 13, 1950, there was held at the American University, Washington, D.C., an Institute on the Structure of the Labor Market. An edited report of the Institute was presented in a book titled *The Impact of the Union* with a subtitle "Eight Economic Theorists Evaluate the Labor Union Movement." The book was published in 1951 by Harcourt, Brace & Co., New York. Dr. Milton Friedman, Professor of Economics, University of Chicago, in his paper "Some Comments on the Significance of Labor Unions for Economic Policy" (pp. 204–34) questioned the economic importance of unions, especially their effect upon wage structure; he believes that unions have taken or been given credit for wage increases that would most likely have occurred without unionism. Dr. Friedman stated:

> "Total union membership is currently (1950) about 16 million, or something over one-quarter of the labor force. On the basis of our preceding analysis, however, it seems likely that many if not most members are in unions that have had only a negligible effect on wage rates. In the

long view, it seems likely that unions have made wage rates significantly different from what they otherwise have been, primarily in construction, railroads, printing trades, and in general the areas in which old-line craft unions are strong. . . . Roughly, then, we might assess the magnitude of unions' effect on the structure of wages by saying that perhaps 10 per cent of the labor force has had its wages raised by some 15 per cent . . ." (Pp. 215–16.)

The other seven eminent economists did not disagree with Dr. Friedman's analysis.

Surprisingly, not by intention and only indirectly, the authors of the CIO book *The Case against "Right to Work" Laws* came to somewhat the same conclusions:

"The economic advance of the less developed states . . . does . . . depend on the expansion of the national economy, in addition to the growth of consumer markets in those states and the development of their natural resources and power potentials.

"Substantial growth in the economic activities of the less developed states, generally, took place between 1939 and 1943.

"The rapid growth of the less developed states in that period was part of the upsurge in production and employment, as the country was lifted out of the depression decade. . . . The economic development of the less developed states since 1939 has been the result of real economic factors at work and the general advance of the National Economy." (Pp. 160 and 162.)

It should be noted that while the CIO book argues that "Right-to-Work" laws had little or nothing to do with the economic improvement of the "underdeveloped states of the South," neither can unions take credit for the economic development because unionism, in the South, has admittedly been weak.

Since wages depend on productivity the following statement of the CIO book is significant because it indirectly admits that other factors (than unionism) are mainly responsible for increased productivity:

> "Productivity depends generally on a company's efficiency of production—on skills of the work-force, the efficiency of the machinery, the flow of work from one operation to another, and on managerial ability. Output per man-hour in the less developed states is probably about equal to that in the more highly industrialized states."

Unions, Today, Perform Many Non-Economic Functions

Judge Carter of the Nebraska Supreme Court brought out a fine point regarding "free riders" but more significantly clearly shows why compulsory unionism should today be opposed because unions, in their functioning, are becoming more and more political:

> "I fail to see any relation, whatever, between compelling union membership and enforcing payments by employees for benefits received from collective bargaining. Assuming that contributions can be compelled for the representation required in securing benefits accruing to non-union employees as well as to those belonging to the union, compulsory union membership exceeds the necessities of the case and compels an employee to join and support an association of persons with whose purposes and concepts he may be in total disagreement. The Constitution protects an individual against legislation having this effect.

> "If an employee is compelled to join a union against his will in order to continue in his employment, he not only pays his share of the cost of the union's bargaining processes, but he is compelled to support many other principles, policies, programs, and activities to which he may not subscribe. Some unions support a form of life insurance which pays death benefits; some support a welfare fund for the benefit of needy members. Some unions maintain a strike fund to

protect employees when on strike, some establish funds to be used in the furtherance of economic and political principles in which an employee may have no confidence. In some instances compulsory membership would compel support, financial and otherwise, of policies which an employee might deem objectionable from the standpoint of free government and the liberties of the individual under it. An employee may neither desire the benefits of such programs nor desire to contribute to their support. He may object to certain programs and activities of the union for reasons of his own and, consequently, not desire to contribute to their promulgation. To compel any employee to make involuntary contributions from his compensation for such purpose is a taking of his property without due process of law.

"We have prided ourselves in this country in the rights of free speech and free thought, rights which have been guaranteed to us by constitutional provision. Compulsory unionism infringes upon these rights and often encroaches upon the right of an individual to be free from coercion by others. To compel him to contribute to the support of economic or political programs adopted by a union, which may be abhorrent to him, is as constitutionally wrong as if similar programs were compelled by the employer. The Fifth Amendment protects against the forced appropriation of one's property for the support of ideals which he may desire to oppose. The right to work and to be compensated therefore is a fundamental principle in our democratic thinking. To force contributions against one's will in the manner here employed is a violation of his fundamental rights and privileges. It is a violation of 'nor be deprived of life, liberty, or property, without due process of law,' contained in the Fifth Amendment of the Constitution of the United States. "Constitutional guarantees exist in fair weather and in foul. They may be asserted by the minority against the majority, and by the individual even against the power of government. They may be asserted by an employee against his employer or a labor union, or both. An employee not only has a right to work, but he has the guaranteed right to have his earnings protected against confiscation against his will. Forcing an employee to join a union and to compel him to financially support principles, projects, policies, or programs in which he does not believe and does not want, is clearly a taking of his property without due process.

"If this be true, the constitutional provision here questioned is declaratory of the rights guaranteed to plaintiffs under the Constitution of the United States and, consequently, is not subject to the attack made upon it by these defendants."[1]

It is repugnant that free American citizens be forced, under compulsory unionism, to make contributions to causes, political or economic, to which they may be opposed in principle or in conscience. The merger of the A.F. of L. and the CIO into one huge labor organization which has as one of its important objectives political action and the use of part of the initiation fees, dues and uniform assessments for that purpose, is one of the strongest arguments, today, against compulsory unionism and the forced political contribution for political purposes to which many members may be opposed. One has only to recall the open political contributions of John L. Lewis, Sidney Hillman, David Dubinsky et al. in former years to realize the inherent danger under compulsory unionism, pointed out by Judge Carter that

"Compulsory unionism infringes upon these rights . . . to compel him (the member) to the support of economic or political programs adopted by a union, which may be abhorrent to him, is as unconstitutionally wrong as if similar programs were compelled by the employer."

An outstanding case of what Judge Carter warns against is that of Mr. Cecil B. deMille, who for refusing to contribute a dollar, assessed by the Union for a political purpose to which Mr. deMille was opposed, was suspended from his union (AFRA) and consequently put off the air. From 1944 to this day Mr. deMille has not been allowed to produce a radio show by reason of his refusal to make

[1]*Robert L. Hanson* v. *Union Pacific Railroad Company*, 71 NW 2d, pp. 543–46.

a forced political contribution. Mr. deMille fought his case through the courts to the Supreme Court of California but was unable to get redress by being reinstated in his union and his job. If this can happen to a man as prominent, powerful and wealthy as Mr. deMille what chance has an ordinary worker to protect himself against abuse under compulsory unionism?

Moral Obligation to Join a Union

Another argument is that "Right-to-Work" laws, because they outlaw compulsory unionism, are immoral since there is a moral obligation to belong to a union. The argument is based upon the assumption that union membership is a necessary and only means to the obtaining of economic justice. This assumption cannot be proved from the requirements of the natural law, from the teaching of theologians or from encyclical teaching.

In an article[1] on the moral obligation to belong to a union, Rev. Francis J. Connell, C.SS.R., Dean of the School of Sacred Theology, Catholic University, stated:

"Is there an obligation on the Catholic worker of joining an accredited union of his particular scope of labor. The late Msgr. John A. Ryan answered this question in the affirmative, with a slight qualification:

" 'While it would be impossible to prove that every wage earner is in all circumstances morally obliged to become a union member, it could easily be shown that some degree of such an obligation rests upon the mass of unorganized workers. In the first place, they cannot obtain just conditions of employment without collective bargaining, which is rarely feasible without organization; in the second place, the unorganized employees in an industry or plant which already contains a union are enjoying benefits for which

[1]*The American Ecclesiastical Review*, Vol. 116, 1947, pp. 429–431.

they have not paid; they are reaping where they have not sown."[2]

"One of the tenets of the Association of Catholic Trade Unionists is that every member is bound to join a bona fide union.

"Explaining this Fr. Oberle says:

" 'The obligation of workers to join a union is still a debated point among the exponents of Christian social teaching. But the arguments drawn from the papal encyclicals and from the writings of authorities on Christian social teaching are strong enough to justify this principle of the ACTU. What kind of obligation it is, and what is its binding force may be hard to determine, but without doubt, justice or charity or both often make membership in a union a duty.'[3]

"On the other hand, Dr. George Clune states:

" 'Labour unions are so well supported and have so strengthened the workers that those who remain outside the ranks may be ignored and their failure to join has not very notably decreased the bargaining power of labour. These facts point to a negative answer to the question; and even the statement of the Sacred Congregation of the Council that the Church in the circumstances (1929) considered the formation of industrial associations of employers and employees "morally necessary" does not assert that there is any positive obligation in conscience on the workers to form and join these unions.'[4]

"Personally, I am inclined to favor Dr. Clune's opinion, as far as a general obligation is concerned. We must be careful not to multiply obligations binding under sin; and I would certainly not tell every worker who happens not to be affiliated with any union: 'You are committing sin if you do not join a union.' Nevertheless, I believe that there are times when, because of certain special circumstances—for

[2]*The Catholic Mind*, XLII, 975 (March 1944), p. 157.
[3]Oberle, J., *op. cit.*, p. 18.
[4]Clune, G., *Christian Social Reorganization* (Dublin: Brown and Nolan, 1940), p. 356.

example, when a small union is in need of every member
it can obtain in order to secure protection from evident
injustice—there would be an obligation of charity on individual workers to affiliate themselves with the organization."

The Church favors many other types of private associa-
tion such as religious Congregations and Orders, as Rev.
Ferdinand Falque in his pamphlet "The True Purpose of
Right-to-Work Laws"[5] so clearly points out:

"The Church has always loved organization, because organization means concerted brotherhood in pursuing that
which is good. But noble and beneficial as are the Church's
own organizations, her religious communities, fraternities,
orders, there is no place in any of them for compulsion.
It is of the essence of their every charter and constitution
that they be embraced freely. Is there no significance in
this for associations that seek to promote economic and
social betterment by means of concerted action? Are not
the unions in the true mind of the Church associations of
free men? How can the stigma of immorality be hurled at
those who advocate freedom above economic utility? The
answers will enable us to see the anti-compulsion laws in a
truer light."

But the Church does not compel membership in such
associations despite the desirability and moral goodness
of these private associations.

The opponents of Right-to-Work confuse the Right-to-
Work with the right of private association. They argue
that since the Right-to-Work is social as well as individual
this right must be exercised only in the private association
of a labor union. It is contended the Right-to-Work is a
conditional and social right which is interpreted to mean
that it can be exercised morally only under the condition
of compulsory unionism. The Right-to-Work and the right
to private association are different not identical rights.
The Right-to-Work can legitimately and morally be exer-

[5]Heritage Foundation, Chicago, Ill.

cised independently of association. The fact that the worker might better exercise the Right-to-Work in a private association doesn't mean that association is an essential and morally necessary condition to the exercise of the right. Father Charles Pridgeon, S.J., Principal of the Catholic Workers College, Oxford University, well stated the argument on this point when he said:

> "Let the unions remember that the right to work comes from God, not from them. Man was born to work and he has an inviolable fundamental right to work and to the means to work. That right was not created by trade unions. Unions are meant to give, not to take away. Yet because a man who has tried to get work has no card, his fellow-men protest. They refuse to work alongside a non-unionist, refuse him sustenance for himself and his family. Of course, this can sometimes be valid, but not in all circumstances."

The famous Philadelphia waterfront priest, Rev. Dennis J. Comey, S.J., while opposing "Right-to-Work" laws[6] does not believe there is a universal moral obligation to belong to a union. He answered the question of "Obligation to Join a Union?" as follows:[7]

> "A man who grapples with the problem of joining a union is not wrestling in a vacuum. His concern find its focus on a specific and identifiable union. His moral obligation must be measured in terms of the union's character, its goals, objectives, purposes and the means adopted to achieve its ends. The issue resolves itself into: 'Am I morally obliged to join this union?'

> "A preliminary observation is in order. Though it may be tabbed as heresy, we dare to insist that a union is not an end in itself, it is a means to an end. Men do not band together and pool their resources merely to form a union. The aim reaches beyond that target. Unionization is an expression of man's social character; it is an exercise of a

[6]*The Philadelphia Catholic Standard and Times*, December 2, 1955.
[7]*Ibid.*, November 18, 1955.

natural right; its professed design is to promote the common good by improving wages and working conditions.

"My letter writing friend gets down to cases. He pictures workers who are receiving all that is due them and guaranteed that this nicer feature represents enduring policy; working conditions are properly tailored to the wage-earners' dignity; adequate protection is assured against the hazards of layoff, sickness, old age. Are these men morally obliged to form or to join a union? The answer is 'No.' Given such circumstances, the demands of justice and charity are properly acknowledged by the employer as an obligation to be honored. The union as a means to attain justice, as a means of persuading or compelling the employer to fulfill his social obligation, is not needed. A cynic might complain that such ideal circumstances are wholly imaginary. Even so, they point up a principle. In these circumstances employes are not obliged to organize or to join a union.

"However, another consideration is subject to opinion and discussion. Should well-treated employes be organized to give supporting help to others who really need joint effort to attain legitimate goals? Admittedly the obligation becomes less compelling. An affirmative answer must depend on evidence that the help supplied would be truly effective, that the principled employer will not be penalized for the sins of others. Proof must be convincing before a moral obligation is laid on the well-treated employes to form or to join a union.

"No moralist will agree that a wage-earner is morally obliged to join a union that is demonstrably corrupt or subversive. A reasonable hope of effecting true reform might allow a man to join such a union. But there is a world of difference between permission and obligation.

"Take another case. Guided by a pagan economic philosophy there are employers who resist any and all workers' petitions. The one redress available is unionization; it becomes a necessary means. In those circumstances the common good demands a personal contribution to solidarity. Meaning a moral obligation to join the union.

"That combination of circumstances explains why we have unionism. And such circumstances, making union organization a necessity, are not wholly imaginary."

A pertinent comparison can be made with the natural right to marry. Every person has the natural right to marry and also the natural right of procreation. This latter right can physically be exercised outside the social and private association of marriage; this would be immoral because God has made the exercise of this right conditional, that is, it can be exercised morally only in the association of a valid and licit marriage. Moreover, marriage must be completely free; if either party to the marriage contract is compelled to enter the association of marriage, the marriage is null and void. I know of no theologian who argues that God has placed an equally strong moral condition on the right to work, namely, that it can be exercised morally only in the association of a union.

Compulsory Unionism in Europe and Canada

The 1950 Pastoral Letter of the bishops of Quebec is frequently quoted as authority to prove a universal obligation to belong to a union. The following quotation is usually cited:

"To fulfill the role which is theirs in the national economy, to promote their professional interests, to realize their legitimate economic and social claims, the workers ought to unite in solid professional organizations. . . . Present circumstances render still more pressing and impervious the obligation of the workers as also of the employers to exercise that right." (*The Catholic Mind,* Nov. 1955.)

If under the peculiar circumstances existing in Quebec, the Hierarchy demanded that Catholic workers join unions, Catholic workers would be bound to obey. However, it cannot be proved that this statement of the Hierarchy of Quebec binds Catholic workers in the United States. Also, economic and social conditions in Quebec are different from those in the United States. What is not pointed out by commentators who quote this Pastoral Letter as authority to prove a moral obligation of American workers to belong to a union, is that the Quebec Hierarchy admonished their working people to join Catholic unions over which the Church has strict control. In Quebec such Catholic unions are possible and practical while in the United States purely Catholic unions are both impossible and impractical. In fact the Quebec bishops pointed out in no uncertain language the danger to Catholics of belonging to a purely neutral union, such as our unions in the United States are. (See p. 61 for full quotation and Appendix D for excerpts.)

It must be pointed out, also, that even if one could prove the moral obligation, under certain circumstances, of belonging to a union, this would not make "Right-to-Work" laws immoral per se, so long as such laws do not prohibit unionism or make unionism difficult in practice. These laws, because they permit voluntary unionism, can be held to be moral because, assuming an obligation to join, they do not hinder the fulfillment of that obligation.

It is interesting to note that in December, 1955, in Scotland, a strike at the Rolls Royce plants in the Glasgow area, called to force an employer to discharge a non-union worker, was broken by a Pastoral Letter of three Scotch Catholic bishops, Archbishop Donald A. Campbell of Glasgow, Bishop James Scanlan of Motherwell and Bishop James Black of Paisley. Father Benjamin L. Masse, S.J., associate editor of *America* magazine commented:[1]

> "Over the years many a strike has been broken by the use of scabs, by publicity, by injunctions or by calling out the militia. For the first time so far as this writer knows a strike has just been broken by a Pastoral Letter. . . . One aspect of the Rolls Royce affair will be of more than ordinary

[1]*America*, Jan. 14, 1956, p. 431.

interest to workers and employers in this country. The strike was called because the company refused to discharge a worker at the request of one of the unions. As punishment for working too much overtime, the union had taken away the man's union card. The strike was called, that is, to enforce a union shop. . . .

"Since at the present time the controversy in this country over right to work laws which render illegal the union shop and all other types of union security continues in its devisive way what the Scotch Bishops had to say on compulsory unionism may be helpful."

In the Pastoral Letter the Scotch bishops outlined the principles that "govern the so-called 'closed-shop' or 100 per cent unionism":[2]

"1. Always we should stand in the first place for the individual's right to work and for his freedom to labour where he will. Men are not born to be slaves.

"2. This freedom is not absolute, but may have to be curtailed when the rights of others are threatened.

"3. Therefore in some factory or group of factories, or even an industry, when it is proved beyond reasonable doubt that the general welfare and protection of the workers demand it, it would not be unlawful to institute the closed-shop.

"4. With the strength of the trade union movement today and the general readiness of employers to co-operate with the trade unions, we believe that the need for the compulsory closed-shop is by no means universal.

"5. Where the closed-shop is instituted, safeguards should be taken to ensure that the rights of the individual are not likely to be jeopardized or workers victimized by some pressure or power group among their fellow workers.

"6. We believe in trade unions and would like to see all our people in industry and at work play an active part in

[2]Pastoral Letter from the Archbishops and Bishops of the Province of Glasgow to the Clergy and Laity of the Province, Advent, 1955.

them; indeed we urge them to do so now more than ever in order that these admirable institutions may be always truly representative and democratic."

While the strike leader was a communist the issue was a clear cut case of compulsory unionism and the attempt by the union to enforce it by a strike, as the *Catholic Times* commented in London:

"The closed shop idea has played into the hands of the Reds giving them power over a man's livelihood through the union card."[3]

The observation of the Scotch bishops that

"With the strength of the trade-union movement today and the general readiness of employers to cooperate with trade unions, we believe the need for the compulsory closed shop is by no means universal."

is equally applicable to the United States and to Europe. That it is "by no means universal" in Europe can be proved by the fact that compulsory unionism is no more common in Western Europe, than in this country. In European countries which protect freedom of association by law there is extended also the right *not* to associate. Belgium, the Netherlands, Austria and Denmark have statutory provisions making contracts which contain a compulsory unionism clause null and void. In Germany, under the 1949 Constitution, compulsory unionism is repudiated. In France, Switzerland, Sweden and Norway compulsory unionism is practically non-existent. In Great Britain, where collective bargaining contracts are not enforceable in court there is much opposition to compulsory unionism. See "A British View of 'Right to Work' Laws" by Sir Alfred Thomson Denning, Lord Justice of Appeal, England, in the September 16, 1955 issue of *U.S. News & World Report*. He said among other things:

"It is reasonable that workmen in a particular industry should wish all their fellow workmen to be members of

[3]NCWC News Service, Dec. 26, 1955.

their own trade-union, because that gives them greater bargaining power, but it leads to the "closed shop" as it is called, where a man has no right to work unless he is a member of a particular trade-union. It is reasonable enough, too, that a trade-union should have means of securing discipline among its members, but this leads to private tribunals where a man can be punished without any recourse to the courts of the law."

(By way of parenthesis, Mr. W. Harrison [a union leader who had been expelled from his union for testifying against compulsory unionism before a Congressional committee] in his pamphlet "Forced Union Membership Steals Your Freedom"[4] makes the following pertinent comment:

". . . With the union shop in operation, a man has to think twice before he objects to anything his union officers are doing. For—don't forget the men who bring the charges against him will try him, too. It's a kangaroo court from beginning to end . . .")

That the English people and even union leaders are opposed to compulsory unionism can be proved from the recent statement of Mr. Charles Geddes, Chairman of the British Trades-Union Congress. He stated:

"I do not believe the trade-union movement of Great Britain can live very much longer on the basis of compulsion. Must people belong to us or starve whether they like our policies or not? Is that to be the future of the movement? No. I believe the trade-union card is an honor to be conferred, not a badge which signifies that you have got to do something whether you like it or not. We want the right to exclude people from our union if necessary and we cannot do that on a basis of 'belong or starve.'"

Even the International Labour Organization in its 1949 Convention No. 87 on "Freedom of Association" defended freedom of association to mean non-membership in a union as well as membership as a condition of employment.

It is significant that the International Labour Organiza-

[4]National Right to Work Committee, Washington 5, D.C.

tion to date has not taken a definitive stand either for or against compulsory unionism. In a report on "Discrimination in the Field of Employment and Occupation" presented to the Governing Body in advance of its meeting in November 1955 on the compulsory unionism problem, the ILO Report had this to say:

> "56. Regarding the justification in themselves of union security provisions, it was shown during the discussion at the International Labour Conference in 1949 leading to the adoption of the Right to Organize and Collective Bargaining Convention, No. 98, that there were two irreconcilable schools of thought. The public attitude on this question varies widely from country to country and is largely determined by the national background and traditions and the way in which trade unions have developed. Moreover, where criticism of these arrangements exists, it is often linked in the public mind with a certain anxiety regarding the propriety of any arrangements which place any representative organization, whether workers, professional persons, manufacturers or traders, in a monopolistic position.

> "57. It is suggested that the question of the justification of these arrangements, as indeed also the parallel question of the prevention of victimization of trade union members, goes beyond the limits of this report and that such questions are best treated as separate items from that of general measures for the prevention of discrimination in employment."

Even the United Nations in its Declaration of Human Rights (1948) in Section 1, Article 20 states:

> "1. Everyone has the right to freedom of peaceful assembly and association.

> "2. No one *may be compelled* to belong to an association." [Emphasis supplied.]

The argument offered to explain the lack of compulsory unionism in Europe is that union security is assured by a strong and old labor movement—that European workers are practically 100 per cent unionized. This is by no means true. Proportionately there are at least as many non-agricultural workers in unions in the United States as in Europe. Moreover, where European unions are economically weaker than those in the same industries in the United States, it is primarily because the European organizations have concentrated on political rather than on economic action ("bread and butter" issues).

Encyclical Teaching

Some argue that voluntary unionism in the form of "Right-to-Work" laws is contrary to the social teaching of the Church. Nowhere in the social encyclicals is compulsory unionism specifically or implicitly demanded, nor do the social encyclicals state that workers have a moral obligation to belong to a union to exercise the Right-to-Work. In fact Pope Pius XI, quoting Pope Leo, states that each individual "is quite free *to join or not*" private associations. Pius XI stated:

> "Moreover, just as inhabitants of a town are wont to found associations with the widest diversity of purposes, which each is quite free to join or not, so those engaged in the same industry or profession will combine with one another into associations equally free for purposes connected in some manner with the pursuit of the calling itself. Since these free associations are clearly and lucidly explained by our Predecessor of illustrious memory. We consider it enough to emphasize this one point: People are quite free not only to found such associations, which are a matter of private order and private right, but also in respect to them 'freely to adopt the organization and the rules which they judge most appropriate to achieve their purpose . . .'"
> (Quad. Anno. par. 87)

It is sometimes argued that compulsory unionism is implied in the social encyclicals because the encyclicals so vigorously defend the right of workers to join unions and so strongly advocate the establishment of these associations to promote the spiritual and material welfare of the workers.

Pius XI stated:

"The rules, therefore, which Leo XIII issued in virtue of his authority, deserve the greatest praise in that they have been able to break down this hostility and dispel these suspicions; but they have even a higher claim to distinction in that they encouraged *Christian Workers* to found mutual associations according to their various occupations, taught them how to do so, and resolutely confirmed in the path of duty a goodly number of those to whom socialist organizations strongly attracted by claiming to be the sole defenders and champions of the lowly and oppressed." (Quad. Anno. par. 31)

"To the Encyclical of Leo, therefore, must be given this credit, that these associations of workers have so flourished everywhere that while, alas, still surpassed in numbers by socialist and communist organizations, they already embrace a vast multitude of workers and are able, within the confines of each nation as well as in wider assemblies, to maintain vigorously the *rights and legitimate demands of the Catholic workers and insist also on the salutary Christian principles of society.*" (Quad. Anno. par. 36. Emphasis added.)

These statements, however, do not prove the universal need for compulsory unionism because under voluntary unionism in this country today, the right of free association and adequate union security is provided by law and proved by experience under these laws.

Organized Social Reconstruction

Some argue that the social reconstruction mentioned in the social encyclicals requires organization of all workers in unions. Father John S. Cronin, S.S., best expresses this point of view in the following statement:

"In view of the broader functions of unions, many moralists now hold that workers have a duty to join unions. The soundest basis for such an opinion is the obligation of all to participate in group action aimed to infuse a proper order in economic life, so that the institutions of society will be directed toward the common good. This institutional reform cannot be achieved by individual effort alone. It is essentially social. In industrial life, it transcends the boundaries of the single plant or industry. Even where an employer pays good wages and has excellent working conditions, there are common problems of economic society in the solution of which labor has both an interest and a duty to participate.

"If the reason for labor organization were merely the achievement of individual rights, undoubtedly it could be argued that where such rights are adequately protected, unions would be unnecessary, much less obligatory. But in the wider pattern of modern life, there are two arguments for unions, even with workers whose employers are imbued with both good will and skill in human relations. The first is the need for positive organization of economic life for the common good. Even unselfish individualism will not achieve such positive order. It may seek good goals, but not in a formal and orderly pattern. Secondly, in view of the power concentration in modern life, there is need for buffer groups to safeguard individual rights. Although a given employer is anxious to protect the rights of his workers, these rights may be invaded as a result of actions taken outside of his sphere of competence. There may be arbitrary action by government or selfish moves by other economic groups. Hence workers in this well-regulated concern would need to act with other workers to protect interests common to all."[1]

If institutional reform is essential for social reconstruction and must be organized, then the organization of

[1]*Catholic Social Problems in Economic Life,* p. 418–19 (1950).

both capital and labor is required. One without the other would be meaningless, except it is anticipated that the "institutional reform" would take the form of a collectivistic social reconstruction in which union labor would be the dominant power, both politically and economically, as happened in Great Britain in 1945. The much misquoted Quebec bishops did not fall into this error; they requested the free organization of employers' unions as well as workers' unions in their plan of social reconstruction. They stated:

> "Present circumstances render still more pressing and impervious the obligation of the workers *as also of the employers* to exercise that right (to form unions)."

Yet in this country the so-called labor priests ignore the great need for the organization of employers into effective unions if there is to be organized institutional social reform. Organized cooperation between labor and capital is of the very essence of social reform. Such organized cooperation, however, would demand a radical change in the attitudes and policies of our neutral unions as they exist and function today in this country. The animating spirit of our neutral unions is unfortunately too secularistic and too materialistic as Father Coogan points out in his article (quoted above). His opposition to compulsory unionism is based upon the fact that association being formative (as the Quebec bishops stress) and our neutral unions being materialistic, both conceptually and in practice, such "association can lead the worker astray to materialism and imbue him with a false concept of life eventually made known by harsh claims, unjust methods and the omission of the collaboration necessary to the common good."

Archbishop Alter of Cincinnati in an address titled "Recent Developments in the Church's Program of Social Order" raises some very penetrating questions regarding the place of our neutral unions in the new social order:

"We must be clear in our minds whether we are to reconcile class interest groups by collective bargaining or by a new principle, viz., mutual function and mutual interest. The latter requires active participation in the industry itself, just as the former makes desirable an independent status outside industry control. In attempting to answer this question, doubt and confusion arise concerning the nature and purpose of labor unions, as they now exist. Can they be classified as functional and vocational groups, as conceived in the mind of the Popes; or are they primarily class conflict and class interest groups? Let me hasten to state that there is no question here concerning the necessity of labor unions under present conditions, but only a question as to whether they are the proper units in the proposed new economic structure."[2]

That the Popes had in mind a cooperative organization of both labor and capital for social reconstruction can be proved by the following quotation of Pius XI, who deplored the fact that while in the forty years between his Encyclical (1931) and that of Leo XIII (1891) much had been done to encourage the formation of workers' unions, practically nothing had been done to establish employers' unions:

"Leo's learned treatment and vigorous defense of the natural right to form associations began, furthermore, to find ready application to other associations also and not alone to those of the workers. Hence no small part of the credit must, it seems, be given to this same Encyclical of Leo for the fact that among farmers and others of the middle class most useful associations of this kind are seen flourishing to a notable degree and increasingly day by day, as well as other institutions of a similar nature in which spiritual development and economic benefit are happily combined.

"But if this cannot be said of organizations which Our same Predecessor intensely desired established among employers

2*Recent Developments in the Church's Program of Social Order.* Address delivered on March 20, 1952, by Most Rev. Karl J. Alter, D.D., LL.D., Archbishop of Cincinnati, at St. Peter's College, Jersey City, N.J.

and managers of industry—and We certainly regret that they are so few—the condition is not wholly due to the will of men but to far graver difficulties that hinder associations of this kind which We know well and estimate at their full value. There is, however, strong hope that these obstacles also will be removed soon, and even now We note with the deepest joy of Our soul, certain by no means insignificant attempts in this direction, the rich fruits of which promise a still richer harvest in the future." (Quad. Anno. par. 37–38)

Our anti-trust laws, however, prevent the establishment of effective employers' unions. It is illogical for those who condemn "Right-to-Work" laws as an undue restriction upon the right of workers to organize not to condemn our anti-trust laws as immoral because they deny employers their natural right to form effective employers' unions. Those who argue that employers are not denied this right because employers have organized trade associations such as the National Association of Manufacturers or the United States Chamber of Commerce overlook the obvious fact that such business associations are not counterparts in power and function of labor unions.

If there is a moral obligation for workers to belong to strong, effective unions to implement social reconstruction, then there is an equally strong obligation for employers to form strong, effective employers' unions.

In my personal opinion, the repeal of our anti-trust laws to permit effective employers' unions (it should be mentioned that labor unions are exempt from anti-trust laws) would be a dangerous step to take before the other more essential measures recommended by the encyclicals were established. The first and by far most important would be a restoration of morals so that both labor and employer associations, being formative, would form their members to a true Christian approach to social reconstruction by the substitution of cooperation for class conflict and by a practical regard for the common good. To depend upon a mechanistic and automatic "Reconstruction" from mere institutional change would bring that over-socialization and depersonalization of the individual that Pius XII so fears. His Holiness called such mechanistic reform "superstition":

> "It is superstition to expect salvation from rigid formulas, materialistically applied to the social order, for this way of thinking attributes to such formulas an almost prodigious power which they cannot have."[3]

Father Leo Brown, S.J., Director of the Institute of Social Order at the University of St. Louis (as quoted by Archbishop Alter), made some very pertinent remarks regarding the fusion of organized labor and organized capital into what in effect would be a collusive monopoly:

> "I find it hard to see where these principles (the principle of subsidiarity of function and the principle of social justice and social charity) compel us to throw the weight of Catholic thought behind a socioeconomic structure, basically composed of organized labor and organized capital, fused together in some way at a second or higher stage of the economic hierarchy. I do not think that such a fusion corresponds to the integration built around the community of action and interest which the encyclicals have in mind. Merely joining a large labor union to a large trade association does not, by the fact of juxtaposition, knit them together. It is entirely conceivable that such a structure would point up class warfare in a much more violent fashion."[4]

[3] *Six Social Documents,* p. 45.

[4] *Recent Developments in the Church's Program of Social Order.* Address delivered on March 20, 1952 by Most Rev. Karl J. Alter, D.D., LL.D., Archbishop of Cincinnati, at Saint Peter's College, Jersey City, N.J.

Is Compulsory Unionism Immoral?

Under particular circumstances, one cannot prove that per se compulsory unionism is immoral just as one cannot prove that voluntary unionism per se is immoral. If Catholic unions were feasible in the United States (a farfetched and improbable supposition) compulsory unionism might be morally required of Catholic workers. In the situation where Catholic unions were impossible or impractical, then a necessary condition for permitting compulsory unionism would be the realistic fulfillment of the following requirements of papal teaching regarding good unionism.

Saint Pius X in "Singulari Quadam" cautioned:

"Furthermore, if Catholics are to be permitted to join the trade unions, these associations must avoid everything that is not in accord, either in principle or practice, with the teachings and commandments of the Church or the proper ecclesiastical authorities. Similarly, everything is to be avoided in their literature or public utterances of actions which in the above view would incur censure."[1]

Pope Pius XI stated:

"With respect to the foundling of these societies, the Encyclical ON THE CONDITION OF WORKERS most fittingly declared that 'workers' associations ought to be so constituted and so governed as to furnish the most suitable and most convenient means to attain the object proposed, which consists in this, that the individual members of the association secure, so far as is possible, an increase in the goods of body, of soul, and of property,' yet it is clear that 'moral and religious perfection ought to be regarded as their principal goal, and that their social organization as

[1]*All Things in Christ—Selected Encyclicals and Documents of St. Pius X.* Compiled and Edited by Rev. Vincent A. Yzermans, p. 193 (The Newman Press, Westminster, Maryland, 1954).

such ought above all to be directed completely by this goal.' For 'when the regulations of associations are founded upon religion, the way is easy toward establishing the mutual relations of the members so that peaceful living together and prosperity will result.' " (Quad. Anno, par. 32)

Closed and union shops, however, could be immoral under certain circumstances. They are immoral when Catholic workers are forced to belong to communist or socialist unions. Such forced membership subjects Catholic workers to an intolerable compulsion of conscience and exposes them to grave spiritual danger. Under such circumstances the worker would be wronged in the exercise of his personal rights and would find especially painful the oppression of his liberty and conscience.

That there are communist unions in the United States is a matter of public record. James P. Mitchell, Secretary of Labor, made the following comment on the Longshoremens' Union in Hawaii:

"he felt it would be a good thing if Jack Hall, I.L.W.U. leader in the Islands, carried out an offer to step out of strike threatened sugar and pineapple negotiations . . . that he considered the I.L.W.U. leadership subversive."

What of the unions which are dominated by gangsters, racketeers and criminals? Is there not grave spiritual danger to the workers compelled to belong to such unions? Father Coogan quotes A. N. Raskin, labor reporter of the New York *Times,* as follows:

"Racketeers have made their way into control of unions from New York to Los Angeles on a scale unparalleled since the repeal of Prohibition . . . The idealism that animated many veteran unionists in the days when each union advance was dearly bought is surrendering to the ethics of the market place at the lowest levels."[2]

[2]"Can Nothing Be Said for State 'Right To Work' Laws?" by John E. Coogan, S.J., reprinted from *The American Ecclesiastical Review,* Vol. CXXXIII, No. 6, Dec. 1955, p. 373–4.

While there are means other than "Right-to-Work" laws which could protect the liberty and conscience of workers, is not voluntary unionism the best check against oppression of liberty and conscience by giving the worker the power not to join or to withdraw if he is a member of such a union?

Father Coogan[3] points out that even the pro-union *Commonweal* magazine commented as follows upon the power of unions over their members:

> "The union still has the power to deprive the man of his rights as a member. It still has the power to make it difficult, if not impossible, for him to find work once he is unemployed. . . . The power over a man's job is the power over his life . . . and so it happens that in one of the freest countries in the world you run into these pockets of tyranny, dictatorship, ruthless and violent absolutism, where men, American men, live and work in a state of fear that can only be compared to life under Communism and Fascism. The paradox is that even decent labor leaders who support every bill designed to protect civil liberties will oppose any attempt to protect the rights of union members, calling it 'an unwarranted interference in the internal affairs of private associations.'"

Would it not seem then that the states have the obligation to enact "Right-to-Work" laws because communist, socialist and racketeering unions are at variance with good morals, with justice and with the welfare of the state? It is no argument that most of our unions are good unions and therefore do not come under indictment. So long as there are some unions and union practices which do come under indictment, then workers should be protected by the minimum protection given by "Right-to-Work" laws by being able not to join or to withdraw. Certainly they should not, in effect, be compelled by law to belong to or remain members of unions which subject them to grave spiritual danger. I would be the first to oppose "Right-to-

[3] *Ibid.*, p. 375.

Work" laws if they unduly restricted and hampered good unionism as well as bad. This, however, cannot be proved either from the "Right-to-Work" laws themselves, which do not prohibit or unduly restrict unionism, or from experience under voluntary unionism.

Membership in Neutral Unions

Saint Pius X, Pope Leo XIII and Pope Pius XI were concerned not merely about the obvious spiritual danger to workers who, by reason of compulsory unionism, are forced to be members of socialist and communist unions, but also about the spiritual danger to workers who join ordinary "neutral" unions such as the CIO and A.F. of L. unions. The popes recommended that whenever possible Catholic workers form Catholic unions; if they cannot do this and are forced to join neutral unions the popes recommended that Catholic workers establish side by side with the neutral unions religious associations of Catholic workers. How serious was the concern of the popes over this matter can be judged by the fact that both Saint Pius X and Pope Pius XI admonished bishops to determine whether or not Catholic workers under their jurisdiction could belong to specific neutral unions.

Saint Pius X stated:

"The Bishops, therefore, should consider it their sacred duty to observe carefully the conduct of all these associations and to watch diligently that the Catholic members do not suffer any harm as a result of their participation. The Catholic members themselves, however, should never permit the unions, whether for the sake of material interests of their members of the union cause as such, to proclaim or support teachings or to engage in activities which would conflict in any way with the directives proclaimed by the supreme teaching authority of the Church, especially those mentioned above. Therefore, as often as problems arise concerning matters of justice or charity, the Bishops should take the greatest care to see that the faithful do not overlook Catholic moral teaching and do not depart from it even a finger's breadth."[1]

Pope Pius XI reiterated at greater length the statement of Saint Pius X:

"This second method (neutral unions) had especially been adopted where either the laws of a country, or certain special economic institutions, or that deplorable dissension of minds and hearts so widespread in contemporary society and an urgent necessity of combating with united purpose and strength the massed ranks of revolutionarists, have prevented Catholics from founding purely Catholic labor unions. Under these conditions, Catholics seem almost forced to join secular labor unions. These unions, however, should profess justice and equity and give Catholic members full freedom to care for their own conscience and obey the laws of the Church. It is clearly the office of bishops, when they know that these associations are on account of circumstances necessary and are not dangerous to religion, to approve of Catholic workers joining them keeping before their eyes, however, the principles and precautions laid down by Our Predecessor, Pius X of holy memory. Among these precautions the first and chief is this: Side by side with these unions there should always be associations zealously engaged in imbuing and forming their members in the teaching of religion and morality so that they in turn may be able to permeate the unions with that good spirit which should direct them in all their activity. As a result, the religious associations will bear good fruit even beyond the circle of their own membership." (Quad. Anno. par. 35)

How could a bishop fulfill his obligation in this matter under legally protected compulsory unionism? Bishop Sidney M. Metzger of El Paso, Texas, instructed Catholic workers in his diocese to withdraw from a communist-

[1] *All Things in Christ—Selected Encyclicals and Documents of Saint Piux X.* Compiled and Edited by Rev. Vincent A. Yzermans, p. 193.

dominated union. Bishop Metzger could not have done this if Texas did not have a "Right-to-Work" law which permitted workers to withdraw from this union without losing their employment. Neither could the Scotch bishops have taken the action they did if Scotland had legally protected compulsory unionism as we do in this country under the Taft-Hartley Act, except in the eighteen states with "Right-to-Work" laws.

Father Coogan[2] remarks that the Catholic labor commentators who quote the 1950 Pastoral Letter of the Quebec bishops ignore or slight that part of the Letter which points out the dangers arising from membership in neutral unions. The Canadian bishops stated:

> "The mass of the workers receive their education almost insensibly from the association to which they belong. The spirit, the vigor which pervades the organized unit proceeds from the mind and the heart of the leaders. That vigor reaches afterwards all the members and conveys to them a particular concept of social life and profession relations. Hence the association is formative. It will be such in a Christian way, if it expressly adheres, in its very constitutions, to the social principles of Christianity, and if the leaders who shape its actions are capable, through their living faith in the authority of Christ and the Church, of submitting their conscience as leaders to those principles. Otherwise the association will lead the worker astray to materialism; it will imbue him with a false concept of life eventually made known by harsh claims, unjust methods, and the omission of the collaboration necessary to the common good."

Father Coogan commenting on this statement observes:

> "Those warnings have abundant current corroboration. Corroborative of the 'formative' influence of the neutral union, Allan S. Haywood, the late Executive Vice-President of the CIO, has explained, 'When you join a union it's kind of like joining a church. You work for nothing else and you

[2]*Ibid.*, p. 372.

believe in nothing else.' Justly then has Fr. Philip Carey, S.J., of the Xavier Labor School, warned us from his abundant experience, 'The philosophy of secularism is a greater present problem to American labor than Communism.' "

In the light of these clear statements of the popes and of the Canadian bishops regarding "neutral" unions and the present Holy Father's strong statement against Catholic cooperation with communists, it is difficult to understand how Father John F. Cronin, S.S., when asked "Would a worker have the moral right to join a Communist-led union?" could answer:

"The moral principle involved here is that of co-operation with persons or causes that are evil. In our imperfect world, we often have to work with groups or individuals whose principles we reject. This is permitted for a good reason, provided we do not partake of any evil cause. A worker might join a bad union because this is the only available way to secure justice at work. Or he may have good hopes that he could help clean up the union." (*The Sign*, Nov. 1955, p. 19)

A more recent statement of Father Cronin is interesting in light of the above quotation. In a letter to the editor of *The Commonweal* for February 17, 1956, page 518, he said:

"Communists in Unions"

Washington, D.C.

To the Editors: I read, and then reread several times, Paul Jacobs' article on "Communists in Unions" (Jan. 20). Several readings did not remove my sense of uneasiness at the article. The author is obviously competent. He cites many facts which are often overlooked by those who discuss the problem. Yet I could not avoid the feeling that important omissions occurred—important enough to modify the conclusions reached.

The impression was left that Communist control of a union does not result in too much damage. Should we overlook in this regard the peddling of the Party Line in union publications? the affording of sinecure jobs for Party stalwarts? efforts to siphon union funds into Communist-favored causes? facilities for recruiting new Party members? and the giving of openings for sabotage and espionage?

Certainly some Party members have been obtained through Red-dominated unions. And the fact that there were apparently no political strikes during the Korean war does not mean that the danger would be absent in a major war.

Again, should we overlook the relatively great influence exercised by key figures in the legal and publicity divisions of the CIO during the 1940's? Surely the curious parallel between CIO policy and Communist policy in many foreign-policy resolutions and statements during that period has some significance. Moreover, the evidence is strong that the prestige of the CIO was used to push certain Communists into critical government positions (e.g., among the Occupation officials in Germany).

In the light of these facts, it would seem that any added push toward dissolution, such as is afforded by use of the Communist Control Act of 1954, would be defensible public policy.

(Rev.) John F. Cronin, S.S.
Asst. Director, Dep't. of Social Action, NCWC.

It should be recalled that Pius XII put under excommunication Catholics who cooperate with Communists. It would be difficult to conceive of any circumstances in the United States today which would justify Catholic workers joining a Communist-led union.

Pope Pius XII was also concerned about the personal liberty and freedom of conscience of the Catholic worker under compulsory social organization. The Holy Father stated:

"Consciences are today also afflicted by other oppressions. Again, access to employment or to places of labor is made to depend upon registration in certain parties or in certain organizations which trace their origin to the labor market. Such discriminations are indicative of a wrong concept of the proper function of labor unions and of their essential purpose, which is the protection of the interests of the wage earner within modern society, which has become more and more anonymous and collectivist.

"In fact, is not the essential purpose of unions the affirmation in practice that man is the subject, and not the object of social relations? Is it not their purpose to protect the individual against the collective irresponsibility of anonymous owners? Is it not to represent the person of the worker against those who are inclined to consider him merely as a productive agent with a determined price value? How, therefore, can they consider it normal that the protection of the personal rights of the worker be more and more in the hands of an anonymous group, working through the agency of immense organizations which are of their very nature monopolies? The worker, thus wronged in the exercise of his personal rights, will surely find especially painful the oppression of his liberty and of his conscience, caught as he is in the wheels of a gigantic social machine.

"Whoever would think that this solicitude of Ours for true liberty is without foundation when We speak, as We do, to that part of the world which is generally called the 'free world' should consider that, even there, first of all real war and then the 'cold war' have forcibly driven social relations in a direction which ultimately curtails the exercise of liberty itself, while, in another part of the world, this tendency has reached the ultimate consequences of its development."[3]

While one cannot contend that this statement can be used as a defense of "Right-to-Work" laws because it was a private allocution and therefore not applicable to specific legislation in a specific country, neither can one contend that as a general statement of principle it does not apply

[3]*Six Social Documents of His Holiness Pope Pius XII*, pp. 54–55. See Appendix F for excerpts from the 1952 Christmas message of Pope Pius XII.

to the United States; that it applies only to Russia and certain socialist countries in Western Europe. The Holy Father seems to warn against such exclusion when he states:

> "Whoever would think that this solicitude of Ours for true liberty is without foundation when We speak, *AS WE DO,* to that part of the world which is generally called the 'free world' should consider that, even there, first of all real war and then the 'cold war' have forcibly driven social relations in a direction which ultimately curtails the exercise of liberty itself . . ." [Emphasis added.]

Is not the United States part of the "free world" and was she not engaged in the real war (2nd World War) and is she not now engaged in the "cold war"?

Although the Pope, in the above statement, does not condemn the closed or union shop neither does he say compulsory unionism is required and that legal restriction on compulsory unionism is immoral. Wherever, as in this country, the security of unions is fully protected by laws which legally guarantee workers the right to join unions without interference from employers, then the protection of the worker against being "wronged in the exercise of his personal rights" and protected against "the oppression of his liberty and of his conscience" by "Right-to-Work" laws cannot be ignored, much less declared immoral.

Pope Leo XIII seemed also to be concerned about the threat to Christian workers under compulsory unionism when he stated:

> "Certainly, the number of associations of almost every possible kind, especially of associations of workers, is now far greater than ever before. This is not the place to inquire whence many of them originate, what object they have, or how they proceed. But the opinion is, and it is one confirmed by a good deal of evidence, that they are largely under the control of secret leaders and that these leaders apply principles which are in harmony with neither Christianity nor the welfare of the States and that, after having

possession of all available work, they contrive that those who refuse to join with them will be forced by want to pay the penalty. Under these circumstances, workers who are Christians must choose one of two things; either to join associations in which it is greatly to be feared that there is danger to religion, or to form their own associations and unite their forces in such a way that they may be able manfully to free themselves from such unjust and intolerable oppression. Can they who refuse to place man's highest good in imminent jeopardy hesitate to affirm that the second course is by all means to be followed?" (Rerum Novarum, par. 74.)

Does the State Have the Right to Regulate Unionism?

In dealing with the moral aspect of "Right-to-Work" laws, touching primarily upon temporal well-being, one should keep in mind that it is a requirement of morality that true competency in such a matter be ascribed to the state, to the effect that it pertains to civic authority to choose and determine *freely, within reason,* the means of safeguarding and promoting civic well-being and good order.

Some well-meaning sociologists seem to think that only the Church can determine moral means of temporal welfare, overlooking the fact that within a wide sphere of reasonable choice, a means is morally justified by the very fact that the state, and frequently the state alone, may determine and has by law or decree a specific means. Without such determination of the state, the means in question may be purely indifferent in relation to morality.

It is a matter of good morality to take into serious practical account the doctrine of *Immortale Dei:*

"The Almighty, therefore, has appointed the charge of the human race between two powers, the ecclesiastical and the civil, the one being set over divine, and the other over human things. Each in its kind is supreme, each has fixed limits within which it is contained, limits which are defined by the nature and special object of the province of each, so that there is, we may say, an orbit traced out within which the action of each is brought into play by its own native right. But inasmuch as each of these two powers has authority over the same subjects—related differently . . . God, who foresees all things, and who is the Author of these two powers, has marked out the course of each in right correlation to the other. . . . There must, accordingly, exist between these two powers, a certain orderly connection, which may be compared to the union of the soul and body in man. The nature and scope of that connection can be determined only, as we have laid down, by having *regard to the nature of each power,* and by taking account of the relative excellence and nobleness of their purpose. One of the two has for its proximate and chief object the well-being of this mortal life; the other the everlasting joys in heaven. Whatever, therefore in things human is of a sacred character, whatever belongs either of its own nature or by reason of the end to which it is referred, to the salvation of souls, or to the worship of God, is subject to the power and judgment of the Church. Whatever is to be ranged under the *civil* and *political* order is rightly subject to the civil authority." (*Immortale Dei,* Nov. 1, 1885, Ass. Vol. 18, p. 161)

It would be difficult to defend the position that in its own field of interests and responsibility the state has no adequate moral means of right determination. If the state determines means contrary to the divine and ecclesiastical means of salvation, then the Church is indeed empowered to establish this fact and oppose itself to such determination of means. But in regard to setting up objectives of civil good of a temporal order such as commonly pertain to sociology and economics, it definitely is within the competency of the state to make moral determination according to its own native and God-given rights.

Father Coogan[1] made the following observation:

"Catholic commentators scorning the Right to Work laws usually seem to pay little attention to the natural rights of the State as a part of the divine plan to provide for the material and temporal needs of families. Those rights—of course a commonplace in the Philosophy of the Schools— imply a divinely imposed obligation upon State governments to pass laws seriously thought conducive to the common good. And as long as those laws are not clearly beyond defense, it ill becomes the friends of union labor to charge dishonorable governmental motives. The State is of course as truly a part of the divine plan as is the Church, despite their belonging to different orders. We Catholics are quick to resent easy imputation of dishonest motivation to churchmen. It is not clear that we are always as careful of the good name of State governments in matters in which those governments are not obviously without justification."

That the state does have the power to regulate unions is amply proved by the following statement of Pope Leo XIII:

"Occasionally there are times when it is proper for the laws to oppose associations of this kind (unions), that is, if they professedly seek after any objective which is clearly at variance with good morals, with justice or with the welfare of the State. Indeed, in these cases the public power shall justly prevent such associations from forming and shall also justly dissolve those already formed." (Rerum Novarum, par. 72)

If the state can justly dissolve or forbid the establishment of unions if they are "at variance with good morals, with justice or with the welfare of the state," then certainly the state can do less, namely, enact "Right-to-Work" laws which do not forbid or dissolve unions but merely prevent compulsory unionism when the state judges compulsory unionism to be "at variance with good morals, with justice or with the welfare of the State."

[1]*Ibid.*, p. 371.

Majority Rule

Some opponents of voluntary unionism argue that when a majority of the workers demand a union shop, it is unjust for the minority to oppose or to be allowed to oppose by "Right-to-Work" laws the will of the majority. They point out that when the majority of voters elect a Democratic President, the Republican minority must obey him. This is exactly what is demanded by "exclusive representation" when the minority in an open shop are compelled to bargain through the union by reason of majority vote. It would be absurd to argue that when a Democratic majority wins an election, the Republican minority are obligated to join the Democratic Party.

Moreover, it must be remembered that what is established for private labor unions, must also apply in the eyes of the law to all private institutions. If the will of the majority can enforce compulsory membership in a labor union, then the will of the majority can enforce compulsory membership of Catholics in a communist organization of teachers, where Catholics are a minority.

Mrs. Elinore M. Herrick, Director of Personnel of the New York *Herald Tribune*, presented "The Case for the Closed Shop" at a symposium conducted by the Academy of Political Science on "The Right to Work." However, she made the following observations on the majority vote in a union:

> "Because the Taft-Hartley Act has long been established it is unrealistic to think that the Taft-Hartley Act has abolished a de facto closed shop. Politically the subject of union monopolies seems too hot to handle. Yet, it seems to me that, with the extension of unionization and compulsory unionism, the monopolies being created thereby will have to be faced before long.

"One aspect of this problem is the fact that, although we speak of determination by majority whether a given union should receive exclusive representation rights, actually a majority of those who vote—not a majority of those in the bargaining unit—decide the issue. That is why during the early Wagner Act days employers urged all employees in the bargaining unit to vote. But they do not all do so. That is also why employers also carved out some mighty strange bargaining units when consenting to an election because they wanted to include the votes of persons they assumed would be anti-union. It seldom worked as planned. After the union is established we pass clearly from any semblance of majority rule to minority rule. Only 15 to 20 percent attend union meetings and decisions are reached chiefly by voice vote. So actually you get the coerced vote of a minority which can make its policy bind all because of the fiction of exclusive bargaining. This hardcore minority can force the granting of some form of compulsory unionization. Even when the government ran the union-shop elections the results were overwhelmingly for the union shop. When the union has the power of a closed or even a union shop, the power delivered to it by a minority is very, very great . . .

"Secondly, I believe that there is today no justification for permitting extension of the closed shop to recently organized plants. Although I have stated the case for the 'closed union' I believe it is incompatible with the growth of unionization under government protection. There is no doubt that the closed shop plus the closed union gives power which too often corrupts."[1]

Mr. W. T. Harrison in his pamphlet *Forced Union Membership Steals Your Freedom,* states:

"In their argument on majority rule the union spokesmen entirely overlook the fact that under the laws of our land the rights of the minority are protected, which they are not in a union shop contract. Thus when one political party wins an election it isn't given the power to kick those

[1]Proceedings of the Academy of Political Science, May, 1954, Vol. XXVI, No. 1, pp. 24 and 30.

opposed to it out of their jobs, or to make them join the winner. The rights of the minority are protected by law, by the Constitution and by the American principles of fairness and justice. After all, the unions are private organizations. They were formed to operate only for the benefit of their members and not for the benefit of all, as government is supposed to do. . . .

". . . The labor unions today want the powers of government but they want them without the responsibilities of government. The labor leaders say that if an individual union member objects to any policy, he can work to have the policy changed and at election time he can vote to change the union officials who have recommended the policy.

"Those of us who know the way unions are really run get a snicker out of such statements, knowing them to be pure 'hog-wash.' Talk about your political machine. Lots of unions make the old-time political bosses look like rank amateurs. The political bosses get thrown out now and then, but the union bosses go on forever—unless, of course, they fall out and fight among themselves.

"It has reached the point where many local unions and local union officers often have little or nothing to say about their own affairs. The officers of the national or international decide things for them . . .

". . . With the union shop in operation, a man has to think twice before he objects to anything his union officers are doing . . . For—don't forget—the men who bring the charges against him will try him, too. It's a kangaroo court from beginning to end." (Pp. 5, 7, 8.)

Economic Growth

Finally, opponents of voluntary unionism maintain that it is immoral because they contend economic growth and progress has been less in states with "Right-to-Work" laws than in states without such laws.

Mr. W. R. Brown, Director of Research, Missouri Chamber of Commerce, said at the symposium on "Right to Work" (p. 49):

". . . I have compared the rate of growth in the right-to-work states with Missouri, a specific state that does not have the right-to-work laws, because that is a question we have been faced with.

"I have found that in several of the right-to-work states this situation exists. I have a copy here if you want the exact statistics. But let me say that in several of the right-to-work states we have found that the rates of wage increase have been greater than in Missouri. And perhaps more significant from the broader economic viewpoint, we found that all save one of the right-to-work states had had much greater economic growth than Missouri on a proportional basis as indicated by retail and purchasing power income . . . I don't believe my reply adequately indicated that in November, 1953, official U.S. Bureau of Labor Statistics revealed the average hourly earnings of production workers in manufacturing was greater in three of the thirteen right-to-work states than in Missouri and six of them showed a greater proportionate wage increase between 1949 and 1953 than did Missouri. Nor, did I make it clear that all of the then thirteen right-to-work states, except North Dakota, showed significant increases in per capital retail sales between 1949 and 1953, and in eleven of the remaining twelve states the percentage increase was greater than in Missouri. This report also shows a similar situation to prevail in regard to disposable income and increase in number of employees in nonagricultural establishments."[1]

The following statistics are pertinent: Total Personal Income of states with "Right-to-Work" laws increased in the period 1940–1954 330.6%, while the total income of states without "Right-to-Work" laws increased 263.4%.

Since 1940, the South (the region where Right-to-Work

[1]Proceedings of the Academy of Political Science, May 1954, Vol. XXVI, No. 1, p. 49.

States are concentrated), has made the greatest economic progress of any region in the country. From 1940 to 1954, the total personal income of the Southern States (Southeast and Southwest) increased 337.2%, as compared to a 247.8% increase for the remainder of the United States. However, it must be pointed out that the South, despite its economic progress since the 1940's, is still economically behind the rest of the nation. Per capita income by region in 1954 indicates the wide variation.

	Per Capita Income by Region		% Change
	1940	1954	
New England	$ 757	$ 1,935	155.6%
Middle East	767	2,000	160.8
Central	629	1,920	205.2
Far West	785	2,094	166.8
Northwest	459	1,583	244.9
Southwest	418	1,544	269.4
Southeast	339	1,233	263.7

In 1954 Mississippi had the lowest per capita income ($873); Delaware with a per capita income of $2,372, Connecticut with $2,361 and Nevada with $2,414 were the highest per capita income states. (Nevada has a "Right-to-Work" law, passed by a direct vote of the people and upheld in 1954 by another direct vote.)

Unionism or lack of unionism has had little to do with economic progress or a lack of it in the South. The South, before the war, was economically backward because of a lack of industrialization and a lack of diversification of farming. In the postwar period both of these weaknesses are being rapidly corrected. The most one can say is that "Right-to-Work" laws have not impeded this postwar progress and I doubt if they have been much of a factor in causing it. This was admitted by the CIO in the book *The Case against the Right-to-Work Laws,* when the authors stated:

"Examination of available data on general economic activity reveals no causal relationship between the adoption of right to work laws and economic progress."[2]

While this statement of the CIO was intended to disprove that "Right-to-Work" laws attract new industries, it does prove that "Right-to-Work" laws have not impeded economic progress.

Professor Frederic Meyers implies that "Right-to-Work" laws had little to do with impeding economic growth. He stated:

"These facts of growth, on a little reflection, should not be surprising. It is the usual view that the development of a stable labor movement is dependent upon the development of an industrial economy. I will not bore you with data on the growth on factory industry in Texas—suffice it to say that in the past twenty years, Texas, only somewhat ahead of the rest of the South, has been transformed from an agricultural to an industrial economy . . ."[3]

Members of the Board of Editors of *U.S. News & World Report* made a survey of the Plantation States (Alabama, Georgia, Louisiana, Mississippi and South Carolina); all five of these states have "Right-to-Work" laws. The results of their survey were published in an article "The Change in Industrial America, Story of What's Happening in the South."[4] The survey shows an economic revolution is going on in the deep South which has caused the dethroning of "King Cotton," the destruction of "sharecropping" and the reconstruction of the Southern economy by diversification of farming and industrialization. One of the authors states:

"The Deep South is living through an upheaval more profound, in many ways, than the Secession.

[2] P. 157.

[3] "The Growth of Collective Bargaining in Texas" (1954 Annual Convention of The Industrial Relations Research Association), pp. 3–5.

[4] Jan. 27, 1956, p. 48.

"This revolution, unlike the first one, is not emotional. It is basic, and it shows every sign of enduring. It is changing the base on which the South makes its living. In the process, traditions, habits, and ways of thinking are being plowed under.

"Even the racial make-up of the Plantation States is being altered. Slowly but surely, the white-Negro ratio is getting closer to the national picture.

"All this has been a long time in coming: maybe 50 years, Southern leaders say; maybe longer. As late as 1938, Franklin D. Roosevelt considered the South to be 'the nation's No. 1 economic problem.' Today the measurable transition from that judgment is striking.

"The Deep South is a long way from becoming the industrial powerhouse of the U.S. There are still an awful lot of poor people, with a history of hardship that goes all the way back to the Civil War.

"But, economically, Southerners are gaining on the rest of the country with lengthening strides.

"In Alabama, Georgia, Louisiana, Mississippi and South Carolina—five 'Plantation States' of the Deep South—personal income, manufacturing output and retail sales are four, five and six times what they were in 1939. Some of these States have been advancing in various economic fields at percentage rates higher than the traditionally industrial North.

"Louisiana, for example, since 1947 has outgained the nation as a whole in value of factory output. The South Carolina textile business has forged ahead of that of Massachusetts. The whole South, including the five Plantation States, tops the country in papermaking."

In an interview, Mr. A. Lee M. Wiggins, rail and industrial leader, commenting on unionism in the South, stated:[5]

". . . there are a lot of people in the South who don't want to join a union. They want to be independent. Even

[5]*U.S. News & World Report,* Jan. 27, 1956, p. 62.

many who join a union want to feel that if they don't like the way it's run they can resign and they won't lose their jobs. And that freedom is right important to the dignity and independence of a lot of people."

Freedom of Contract

The argument is advanced that neither the "Right to Work" nor the right of contract is absolute (which, of course, is true)—that both rights are encumbered by many conditions. Specifically it is contended that freedom of contract is denied to the employer (as well as to employees) when he is forbidden by law to enter into a compulsory union contract, especially when the contract is entered into voluntarily by the employer with a majority of his employees. What is ignored is that neither the employer nor the union, except in extreme circumstances, has the right to deprive even a minority of its right of non-association. This is doubly true when 100 per cent unionism is possible under voluntary unionism as it is in this country.

Again the basic issue is not unionism or security of unionism but voluntarism *vs.* compulsion.

Mr. Joseph L. Lenihan in a letter to the Editor of *The Record*[1] gives an excellent rebuttal to this argument:

"With further reference to the subject of 'right to work' laws, I shall appreciate the opportunity to make response to the letter of Rev. William J. Smith, S.J., which appeared in the June 17 issue of your paper.

"First: Father Smith states that the immorality of 'right to work' laws consists in 'the deprivation by the State of the exercise of the right of freedom of contract to both management and unions.' Would Father Smith contend that freedom of contract is an absolute right?

[1]*The Record* (published by the Archdiocese of Louisville, Ky.), July 1, 1955.

"If so, he is in the position of defending the right of an employer to exact from his employees an obligation to abstain from union membership. Since I am confident that Father Smith does not wish to be in that position, he must concede that the right of freedom of contract is subject to reasonable limitations. The question is, then, whether or not the limitations imposed by 'right to work' laws are reasonable. I submit that they are.

"Protection from Power

"Under absolute freedom of contract, (a) if the employer is stronger than the union, the worker can be forced to abstain from union membership; or (b) if the union is stronger than the employer, the worker can be forced to join the union. Laws outlawing the 'yellow dog' contract protect the worker from the excessive power of the employer. 'Right to work' laws protect him from the excessive power of the union. The worker is made a free man—free to join the union if he wishes, free to remain a non-member if that is his inclination.

"Second: Concern that 'right to work' laws will deprive management of its 'right' to enter into union-shop agreements is unrealistic. Management does not seek union-shop agreements. Such agreements are sought by the unions, and in most cases they are forced upon the unwilling employer by the threat of strike. Union-shop agreements are products of union power, not employer choice.

"Third: Father Smith says that more than five million workers and their employers in fourteen hundred industries work under union-shop agreements, and that 'the passage of a Right-to-Work Law in the States where these American citizens carry on their industrial relations would make each of them a criminal.' As for employers, any 'right to work' law which attempted to impose any kind of criminal penalties retrospectively would run afoul of the prohibitions against *ex post facto* laws contained in Article I, Section 9, Clause 3, and Article I, Section 10, of the Federal Constitution.

"As for workers, 'right to work' laws do not impose sanctions against them. The passage of such laws would not require even one of the five million union members to give up his union membership. Such laws would simply restore the individual worker's freedom to choose between membership and non-membership.

"Appeal for Reasoned Views

"Fourth: Father Smith states that the union shop is morally indifferent 'and becomes good or evil according to its use and circumstances.' If this be true, then the difference which exists between Father Smith and those who share his views, on the one hand, and me, on the other, must be accounted for by the difference in our evaluations of those uses and circumstances.

"I inquire whether or not my opponents sought the reasoned views of informed proponents of these laws before pronouncing such laws to be immoral. If not, I assert that their pronouncements of immorality were improvidently made.

"A pronouncement by Catholic Bishops and theologians that a law is 'immoral' constitutes a virtual anathema which stifles the free discussion of the merits of the law in Catholic circles.

"On the strength of such pronouncements, some Catholic organizations, without independent study or certain knowledge of the facts, are prone to adopt resolutions condemning the proposed law. The controversy soon disintegrates into a propaganda battle of slogans, word-play and name-calling, and the merits are completely lost sight of. My purpose was and is to have removed this bar to reasoned discussion."

Conclusion

As a conclusion, I could offer no better statement that the following excerpts taken from Samuel Gompers' last address as president to the American Federation of Labor's convention, held at El Paso, Texas, in 1924. His successors in the labor movement today would do well to heed the wise and calm advice of the "Grand Old Man" of Labor. If Mr. Gompers, in the period when unionism was relatively weak did not demand compulsion as necessary for union security but recommended voluntarism as the very cornerstone of labor's structure, then it ill befits the union leaders of today protected by law and with a strong union movement at their back to foreswear the principle of voluntarism for the totalitarian principle of compulsion.

Mr. Gompers said:[1]

". . . In 1886 a national labor conference was called. This time it was designated a trade union conference to be composed of representatives of trade unions and to consider trade union problems. The deliberations of that conference resulted in the formation of our present American Federation of Labor with which the old Federation of Trades and Labor Unions was merged. This new Federation recognized only the trade union card as a credential and proposed to deal primarily with economic problems. It was an organization that had no power or authority except of a voluntary character. It was a voluntary coming together of unions with common needs and common aims. That feeling of mutuality has been a stronger bond of union than could be welded by an autocratic authority. Guided by voluntary principles our Federation has grown from a weakling into the strongest, best organized labor movement of all the world. So long as we have held fast to voluntary principles and have been actuated and inspired by the spirit of service, we have sustained our forward progress and we have made our labor movement something to be respected and accorded a place in the councils of our Republic. Where we have blundered into trying to force a policy or a decision, even though wise and right, we have impeded, if not interrupted, the realization of our aims.

"Men and women of our American trade union movement, I feel that I have earned the right to talk plainly with you. As the only delegate to that first Pittsburgh convention who

[1]*Christian Economics,* Feb. 7, 1956.

has stayed with the problems of our movement through to the present hour, as one who with clean hands and with singleness of purpose has tried to serve the labor movement honorably and in a spirit of consecration to the cause of humanity, *I want to urge devotion to the fundamentals of human liberty—the principles of voluntarism. No lasting gain has ever come from compulsion. If we seek to force, we but tear apart that which, united, is invincible.* There is no way whereby our labor movement may be assured sustained progress in determining its policies and its plans other than sincere democratic deliberation until a unanimous decision is reached. This may seem a cumbrous, slow method to the impatient, but the impatient are more concerned for immediate triumph than for the education of constructive development.

"Understanding, patience, highminded service, the compelling power of voluntarism have in America made what was but a rope of sand, a united, purposeful, integrated organization, potent for human welfare, material and spiritual. I have been with this movement since the beginning, for I have been given the privilege of service that has been accorded but few. Nor would that privilege have continued open to me had not service to the cause been my guiding purpose. Events of recent months made me keenly aware that the time is not far distant when I must lay down my trust for others to carry forward. When one comes to close grips with the eternal things, there comes a new sense of relative values and the less worthy things lose significance. As I review the events of my sixty years of contact with the labor movement and as I survey the problems of today and study the opportunities of the future, *I want to say to you, men and women of the American Labor movement, do not reject the cornerstone upon which labor's structure has been builded—but base your all upon voluntary principles and illumine your every problem by consecrated devotion to that highest of all purposes—human well-being in the fullest, widest, deepest sense.*" [Emphasis added.]

Summary

The moral argument against "Right-to-Work" laws is based upon the premise that compulsory unionism is necessary today to provide reasonable security for the continued existence and efficient functioning of labor unions. Put another way, the argument would run as follows: Workers have a natural right to join a union; union security clauses are a necessary means for the exercise of this right of association and therefore "Right-to-Work" laws are immoral because they prohibit the use of this necessary means and therefore nullify the right to join a union.

The proponents of voluntary unionism answer this argument by denying the premise. If the premises were true then one would have to grant that "Right-to-Work" laws are unjust. But if this premise is urged as indicating merely considerable union security or easy union security, then there are other considerations that permit excluding compulsory unionism. Union security clauses are an effective way to exercise the right of unionism but they are not a necessary means. No one has proved that compulsory unionism is the only reasonable and normal means of security for labor unions today. The protective labor laws of both the Federal and state governments can, should and do give adequate and reasonable security to unions today in the United States.

It should be emphasized that the right not to join is a necessary corollary of the right to join, for without a right not to join there can be no such thing as a right to join. Freedom rests on choice, and where choice is denied freedom is destroyed as well.

The Supreme Court has recognized the affirmative and negative sides of constitutional rights in the case *Board of Education* v. *Barnette*, 319 U.S. 624,633 (1943), where the Court pointed out that freedom of speech carries with it the freedom to remain silent.

Voluntarism is at the foundation of our Christian and constitutional heritage. To deny it in an area as broad and important as labor, could so weaken that foundation as to threaten all our cherished natural and constitutional rights. This would be "selling our heritage for a mess of pottage."

Rev. Robert Anderson, Editor of the *Nevada Register*, Nov. 12, 1954, made a significant comment and recommendation when he stated:

> "It seems to me, that 'union solidarity' is capable of being distorted dangerously . . . just as are patriotism and even religious enthusiasm. This of course does not make it evil. This rebuff, by the people of Nevada, to further 'union solidarity' does not, by any means, herald the end of unionism here. . . . But it should do one thing . . . it should imbue the active, intelligent, Christian workers with a desire to participate in the life of their union . . . in order to penetrate it with a new spirit and help not only themselves but everyone with a truer understanding of the requirements of social justice . . . in relation to the rights and wellbeing of the whole community . . ."

It ill befits the United States as the one place in the world where the personal worth, dignity and liberty of the individual is a cherished tradition, to set the example of compulsion where voluntarism is not merely possible but practical and effective. Experience proves that union leaders can "sell" good unionism on a voluntary basis.

Professor Meyers is witness to this when he commented:

> "Proponents of legal restrictions on union security frequently argue that unions ought to 'sell' prospective members on the value of union membership, rather than rely on compulsion. The evidence indicates that Texas unions have been able to do this. For example, our estimates of the number of workers covered by agreements with the CIO unions in Texas correspond very closely with estimates made by state CIO officials, in their confiding and conservative moments, of membership of CIO unions in Texas. That implies that almost all workers under contract are union members."

Errata—On pages 93, 102, and 115, the headings for Appendix D and F were transposed.

Appendix D is "Excerpts from the Christmas Message of His Holiness, Pope Pius XII."

Appendix F is "Excerpts from THE PROBLEM OF THE WORKER IN THE LIGHT OF SOCIAL DOCTRINE."

Appendices to

THE CASE FOR
RIGHT-TO-WORK LAWS
A Defense of
Voluntary Unionism

by

REV. EDW. A. KELLER, C.S.C.

93

APPENDIX A
North Carolina Right-to-Work Law

Following is the text of the North Carolina Right-to-Work Law. It has been upheld both by the Supreme Court of North Carolina and by the Supreme Court of the United States.

AN ACT

AN ACT TO PROTECT THE RIGHT TO WORK AND TO DECLARE THE PUBLIC POLICY OF NORTH CAROLINA WITH RESPECT TO MEMBERSHIP OR NON-MEMBERSHIP IN LABOR ORGANIZATIONS AS AFFECTING THE RIGHT TO WORK; TO MAKE UNLAWFUL AND TO PROHIBIT CONTRACTS OR COMBINATIONS WHICH REQUIRE MEMBERSHIP IN LABOR UNIONS, ORGANIZATIONS OR ASSOCIATIONS AS A CONDITION OF EMPLOYMENT; TO PROVIDE THAT MEMBERSHIP IN OR PAYMENT OF MONEY TO ANY LABOR ORGANIZATION OR ASSOCIATION SHALL NOT BE NECESSARY FOR EMPLOYMENT OR FOR CONTINUATION OF EMPLOYMENT AND TO AUTHORIZE SUITS FOR DAMAGES.

The General Assembly of North Carolina do enact:

Section 1. The right to live includes the right to work. The exercise of the right to work must be protected and maintained free from undue restraints and coercion. It is hereby declared to be the public policy of North Carolina that the right of persons to work shall not be denied or abridged on account of membership or non-membership in any labor union or labor organization or association.

Section 2. Any agreement or combination between any employer and any labor union or labor organization whereby persons not members of such union or organization shall be denied the right to work for said employer, or whereby such membership is made a condition of employment or continuation of employment by such employer, or whereby any such union or organization acquires an employment monopoly in any enterprise, is hereby declared to be against the public policy and an illegal combination or conspiracy in restraint of trade or commerce in the State of North Carolina.

Section 3. No person shall be required by an employer to become or remain a member of any labor union or labor organization as a condition of employment or continuation of employment by such employer.

Section 4. No person shall be required by an employer to abstain or refrain from membership in any labor union or labor organization as a condition of employment or continuation of employment.

Section 5. No employer shall require any person, as a condition of employment or continuation of employment, to pay any dues, fees, or other charges of any kind to any labor union or labor organization.

Section 6. Any person who may be denied employment or be deprived of continuation of his employment in violation of Sections 3, 4, and 5 or of one or more of such Sections, shall be entitled to recover from such employer and from any other person, firm, corporation or association acting in concert with him by appropriate action in the courts of this State such damages as he may have sustained by reason of such denial or deprivation of employment.

Section 7. The provisions of this Act shall not apply to any lawful contract in force on the effective date hereof but they shall apply in all respects to contracts entered into thereafter and to any renewal or extension of any existing contract.

Section 8. If any clause, sentence, paragraph or part of this Act or the application thereof to any person or circumstance, shall, for any reason, be adjudged by a court of competent jurisdiction to be invalid, such judgment shall not affect, impair, or invalidate the remainder of this Act, and the application thereof to other person or circumstances, but shall be confined to the part thereof directly involved in the controversy in which such judgment shall be rendered and to the person or circumstance involved.

Section 9. All laws and clauses of laws in conflict with this Act are hereby repealed.

Section 10. This Act shall be in full force and effect from and after its ratification.

APPENDIX B
Algoma Plywood vs. Wisconsin Board

To reflect the holding of the Supreme Court that Section 8(3) of the Wagner Act does not exclude the states from enacting and enforcing measures regulating compulsory unionism, there is the following language from *Algoma Plywood Co.* v. *Wisconsin Board,* 336 U.S. 301, 305–307 (1949):

"The term 'unfair labor practice' is not a term of art having an independent significance which transcends its statutory definition. The States are free (apart from preemption by Congress) to characterize any wrong of any kind by an employer to an employee, whether statutorily created or known to the common law, as an 'unfair labor practice.' At the time when the National Labor Relations Act was adopted, the courts of many States, at least under some circumstances, denied validity to union-security agreements. See 1 Teller, Labor Disputes and Collective Bargaining § 170 (1940). Here Wisconsin has attached conditions to their enforcement and has called the voluntary observance of such a contract when those conditions have not been met an 'unfair labor practice.' Had the sponsors of the National Labor Relations Act meant to deny effect to State policies inconsistent with the unrestricted enforcement of union-shop contracts, surely they would have made their purpose manifest. So far as appears from the Committee Reports, however, § 10(a) was designed, as its language declares, merely to preclude conflict in the administration of remedies for the practices proscribed by § 8. The House Report, after summarizing the provisions of the section, adds, 'The Board is thus made the paramount agency for dealing with the unfair labor practices described in the bill.' H. R. Rep. No. 969, 74th

Cong., 1st Sess. 21. See also the identical language of H. R.
Rep. No. 972, 74th Cong., 1st Sess. 21 and H. R. Rep. No.
1147, 74th Cong., 1st Sess. 23. And the Senate Report de-
scribes the purpose of the section as 'intended to dispel
the confusion resulting from dispersion of authority and
to establish a single paramount administrative or quasi-
judicial authority in connection with the development of
the Federal American law regarding collective bargaining.' S. Rep. No. 573, 74th Cong., 1st Sess. 15.

"The contention that § 10(a) of the Wagner Act swept
aside State law respecting the union shop must therefore
be rejected. If any provision of the Act had that effect, it
could only have been § 8(3), which explicitly deals with
membership in a union as a condition of employment. We
now turn to consideration of that section.

"Section 8(3) provides that it shall be an unfair labor
practice for an employer

" 'By discrimination in regard to hire or tenure of employment or any term or condition of employment to
encourage or discourage membership in any labor organization: *Provided,* That nothing in this Act . . . or in
any other statute of the United States, shall preclude an
employer from making an agreement with a labor organization . . . to require as a condition of employment
membership therein, if such labor organization is the
representative of the employees as provided in Section
9(a), in the appropriate collective bargaining unit cov-
ever by such agreement when made.'

"It is argued, therefore, that a State cannot forbid what
§ 8(3) affirmatively permits. The short answer to that is
that § 8(3) merely disclaims a national policy hostile to the
closed shop or other forms of union-security agreement.
This is the obvious inference to be drawn from the choice
of the words 'nothing in this Act . . . or in any other
statute of the United States,' and it is confirmed by the
legislative history."

APPENDIX C
Wagner Act vs. Taft Hartley Act
WAGNER ACT—1935

Section 8 (3)—"By discrimination in regard to hire or tenure of employment or any term or condition of employment to encourage or discourage membership in any labor organization: Provided, that nothing in this Act, or in the National Industrial Recovery Act . . . as amended from time to time, or in any code or agreement approved or prescribed thereunder, or in any other statute of the United States, shall preclude an employer from making an agreement with a labor organization (not established, maintained, or assisted by any action defined in this Act as an unfair labor practice) to require as a condition of employment membership therein, if such labor organization is the representative of the employees as provided in section 9 (a), in the appropriate collective bargaining unit covered by such agreement when made."

PREVENTION OF UNFAIR LABOR PRACTICES

Section 10 (a)—Board empowered to prevent any person from engaging in any unfair labor practice; such power shall be exclusive and not affected by any other means of adjustment or prevention.

TAFT-HARTLEY—1947

Section 8 (a) (3)—Same as 1935 Act except this addition:

"Provided, That nothing in this Act, or in any other statute of the United States, shall preclude an employer from making an agreement with a labor organization (not established, maintained, or assisted by any action defined in section 8 (a) of this Act as an unfair labor practice) to require as a condition of employment membership therein on or after the thirtieth day following the beginning of such employment or the effective date of such agreement, whichever is the later, (i) if such labor organization is the representative of the employees as provided in section 9 (a), in the appropriate collective-bargaining unit covered by such agreement when made; and (ii) if, following the most recent election held is provided in section 9 (e) the Board shall have certified that at least a majority of the employees *eligible to vote* in such election have voted to authorize such labor organization to make such an agreement:

"Provided further, That no employer shall justify any discrimination against an employee for nonmembership in a labor organization (A) if he has reasonable grounds for believing that such membership was not available to the employee on the same terms and conditions generally applicable to other members, or

"(B) . . . that membership was denied or terminated for reasons other than the failure of the employee to tender the periodic dues and the initiation fees uniformly required as a condition of acquiring or retaining membership."

PREVENTION OF UNFAIR LABOR PRACTICES

Section 10 (a)—Same as 1935 Act except—"exclusive" omitted.

Board may cede jurisdiction in unfair labor practice cases to State boards, provided they conform to national policy, except in mining, manufacturing, communications, or transportation industries not predominantly local in character.

APPENDIX D

Excerpts from

THE PROBLEM OF THE WORKER
in the light of the Social Doctrine of the Church

JOINT PASTORAL LETTER
OF THEIR EXCELLENCIES THE ARCHBISHOPS
AND BISHOPS
OF THE
CIVIL PROVINCE OF QUEBEC

We, By The Grace Of God And Of The Apostolic See, Archbishops And Bishops Of The Civil Province Of Quebec:

To the secular and regular clergy, to the religious communities, and to all the faithful of our dioceses, health and benediction in Our Lord:

SALVATION CANNOT COME FROM PRODUCTION AND ORGANIZATION ALONE

One would say that humanity of today which has had the ingenuity to construct the marvelous and complex machinery of the modern world, subjugating to its service the tremendous forces of nature, now appears incapable of controlling their course, as if the rudder had slipped from its hands, and thus finds itself in danger of being mastered and overpowered by these same forces.

This lack of control of itself ought to suggest to men, who are its victims, not to expect salvation solely from the techniques of production and organization. This technique, provided it be bound up with, and directed toward, an improvement and assertion of true human values, can, indeed, contribute to a notable degree to the solution of the grave and widespread problems besetting the modern world; but in no case—oh! how We wish that all men both on this continent as well as those beyond the sea would come to realize this fact—will technical progress by itself avail in fashioning a world free of misery!

TWO FALSE WAYS

Unfortunately, it might be said, especially in the present case of very widespread miseries, that mankind today is no longer capable of reducing this duality into unity, namely, this necessary adaptation of the general order to the concrete and ever-diversified conditions not only of the individuals but also of the peoples whom one wishes to help.

Salvation is either committed by men to some order which is rigorously uniform and inflexible, and on a world-scale—to a system that must necessarily produce results with the certainty of a tried and proved medicine—to a new social formula reduced to cold, theoretical terms—or, on the other hand, rejecting such general prescriptions, they entrust salvation to the spontaneous forces of the natural instinct in man to preserve life and, in the best hypothesis, to the sentimental impulses of individuals and of peoples, without concerning themselves as to whether the overthrow of the existing order might follow as a consequence of such a course of action, and however evident it might be that salvation cannot be born of chaos.

Both these ways are false, and are far from reflecting the wisdom of God, Who is the first and the exemplary alleviator of human misery. It is superstition to expect salvation from rigid formulas, materialistically applied to the social order, for this way of thinking attributes to such formulas an almost prodigious power which they cannot have; while, on the other hand, to base one's hopes exclusively on the creative forces of the instinct to preserve life which is in each individual is contrary to the designs of God, Who is the Lord of the existing order.

We wish to draw the attention of those who offer themselves as benefactors of these peoples to both these errors,
but particularly to the superstition which would hold for
certain that salvation ought to spring from the organization
of men and of material things into an intimate unity
capable of the highest productive capacity.

If men succeed—so they think—in coordinating the
forces of man and the resources of nature into a single
organic mass, spread out to assure the highest possible
and an ever-increasing productive capacity, by means of
an organization designed and made operative with the
most minute attention given to its important features as
well as its smallest details, then every kind of desirable
benefits will spring forth from such an organization: prosperity, security for the individual and peace.

SOCIAL LIFE CANNOT BE CONSTRUCTED AFTER THE MANNER OF A GIGANTIC INDUSTRIAL MACHINE

One knows where to look for the technologist's point of
view in social thought: namely to the gigantic enterprises
of modern industry. We do not intend here to pronounce
judgment on the necessity, utility and disadvantages of
forms of production such as these. Indubitably, they are
marvelous realizations of the inventive and constructive
genius of the human spirit. Deservedly are these enterprises held up for world-wide admiration which, following
norms which have been maturely considered, succeed both
in production and in management in coordinating and in
uniting the forces of men and of matter. And the present
age may take legitimate pride in the stable way in which
these enterprises are organized and not infrequently in
the wholly novel and characteristic beauty of their external
set-up. But what must be denied is that these forms either
can or should avail as a general model according to which
modern social life should be arranged or with which it
should be made to conform.

It is, above all, a clear principle of wisdom that all progress is truly such only if it knows how to add new conquests to old, to join new benefits to those already acquired in the past—in a word, if it knows how to profit by experience. Now, history teaches that other forms of national economy have always had a positive influence upon the entire social life, an influence which benefited both the essential institutions—such as the family, the state and private property—and those institutions formed by voluntary association. We point out by way of example the undeniable advantages which have been realized wherever agricultural enterprise or that involving the crafts has predominated.

Unquestionably, modern industrial enterprise, too, has had its beneficial results; but the problem which presents itself today is this: "Will a world in which the only economic form to find recognition is a vast productive system, be equally capable of exerting a happy influence upon social life in general and upon the three above-mentioned fundamental institutions in particular?"

We must answer that the impersonal character of such a world is in contrast with the wholly personal inclination of those institutions which the Creator has given to human society. In fact, marriage and the family, the State and private property tend of their very nature to form and to develop man as a person, to protect him and to render him capable of contributing, through his own voluntary collaboration and personal responsibility, to the likewise personal maintenance and the development of social life. The creative wisdom of God remains, therefore, alien to that system of impersonal unity which outrages the human person, the origin and very purpose of social life, and in its innermost essence the very image of God.

THE "DEPERSONALIZATION" OF MODERN MAN

At the present time, unfortunately, it is not a question of mere hypotheses and predictions, for this sad condition is already with us; wherever the demon of organization invades and tyrannizes man's mind, there are at once revealed the signs of the false and abnormal orientation of social development. In many countries the modern State is becoming a gigantic administrative machine. It extends its influence over almost every phase of life. It would like to subject to its administration the entire range of the political, economic, social and intellectual fields, including even the birth and the death of its subjects.

No wonder, then, if in this atmosphere of impersonality, which tends to penetrate and to encompass life in its entirety, the meaning of the common good is diminished in the conscience of individuals, and if the state loses more and more its original character of a community of morally responsible citizens.

In this fact is to be discovered the origin and the source of that current which is submerging modern man under its tide of anguish: his "depersonalization." In large measure his identity and his name have been taken from him; in many of the most important activities of life he has been reduced to a mere object of society, since society itself is being transformed into an impersonal system, into a lifeless organization of forces.

EFFECTS OF THE WIDESPREAD NEGLECT OF THE HUMAN PERSON

If anyone should still harbor doubts about this state of affairs, let him turn his gaze upon the teeming world of misery, and let him ask the ever so diversified classes of needy people what answers society is wont to give them, directed as society now is towards the neglect of the human personality.

Let him ask the ordinary poor man, destitute of every resource, whom one encounters so frequently in cities, in towns and in rural areas alike. Let him ask the impoverished head of a family, a constant visitor to a Relief Agency, whose children cannot wait for the distant and vague compensations of a golden age which is always on its way. Let him put the question, too, to a whole nation whose standard of living is inferior or very low, and which, while being associated in the family of nations side by side with its fellow men who enjoy a sufficient or even an abundant way of life, is waiting in vain from one international congress to another for a stable improvement of its lot in life.

What is the answer which modern society often gives to the unemployed person, who presents himself at an employment office, disposed, perhaps, through habit to receive a new disappointment, but not resigned to the immerited fate of being considered useless? And what is the response that is given to a people who, despite all its efforts and exertions, has not succeeded in freeing itself from the atrophying clutches of mass unemployment?

For a long time now the constant answer which society has given to all these poor people is that their case cannot be handled on a personal and individual basis, but that the solution must be found in an order yet to be established —in a system which will embrace all, and which, without any essential prejudice to liberty, will bring men and matter to a more unified and growing strength of action, by availing itself of an ever more extensive utilization of technological progress. When such a system will have been realized, they say, the prosperity of all men will automatically ensue; a constantly rising standard of life and full employment will be realized everywhere.

Though We are far from believing that the constant references to the future mighty organization of men and matter is a mean diversion invented by those who do not want to help, and even recognizing that it may be a firm and sincere promise, calculated to instill confidence, yet We do not see upon what serious foundations this promise can rest, since lessons gleaned from experience up to the present moment lead one rather to a sceptical attitude toward the chosen system. This scepticism is, moreover,

justified by a kind of vicious circle in which the pre-
ordained and the method adopted revolve one about the
other without ever meeting and being reconciled.

In fact, in those places where one wishes to guarantee
full employment with a constant rise in the standard of
living, one may well pose the anxious question as to the
degree to which expansion is possible without provoking
a catastrophe and, above all, without bringing in its wake
mass unemployment. It seems, therefore, that efforts should
be made to attain the highest possible level of employment,
but at the same time means must be sought to insure its
stability.

No sense of confidence can, therefore, brighten a pano-
rama such as this, over which hovers the spectre of that
insoluble contradiction. Nor will there be any escape
from its spiral, if men continue to depend solely upon the
factor of the highest possible production. One must no
longer consider the ideas of the standard of living and of
employment of labor as purely quantitative factors, but
rather as human values in the full sense of the word.

Whoever, therefore, would furnish assistance to the
needs of individuals and peoples cannot expect salvation
to come from an impersonal system of men and matter, no
matter how vigorously developed in its technological
aspects. Every plan or program must be inspired by the
principle that man as the subject, guardian and promoter
of human values, is more important than mere things,
that he is more important even than the applications of
technological progress, and that, above all, it is imperative
to preserve from an unwholesome "depersonalization" the
fundamental forms of the social order, which We have just
mentioned, and to use them to create and to develop
human relationships.

If the social forces are directed towards this end, they
will not only realize one of their natural functions, but
they will contribute in great measure towards the relief
of the needs of the movement. For these forces of society

have the task of promoting full and reciprocal solidarity among individuals and among peoples. . . .

. . . Such results, however, will not be produced by a mechanical arrangement. Human society is not a machine, and must not be made such, not even in the economic field. Rather, one must always employ the human personality and the individuating characteristics of nations as the natural and the basic fulchrum around which all efforts must revolve in striving to attain the end of the public economy, which end is to insure a stable sufficiency of goods and of material services, directed in turn towards improving moral, cultural and religious conditions. Hence, solidarity and the desired improvements in the proportionment of the living conditions and employment ought to be brought about in the various regions, relatively extensive though they be, where the nature and the historical development of the peoples concerned can more easily offer a common basis for attaining this goal.

ANGUISH OF CONSCIENCE IN MODERN SOCIETY

However, economic difficulties are not the only ones under which man suffers in present-day society. Often connected with these arise difficulties of conscience, especially for the Christian, anxious to live according to the dictates of the natural and the divine law. Those who maintain the impersonal idea of society are condemning to interior anguish that very conscience upon which, in great part, depends the cure for our ills and our salvation itself. And this perhaps is the widest possible deviation from the Divine plan that man is realizing in his efforts to help his fellow man.

Indeed, modern society, which wishes to foresee and to organize everything, because of its mechanical concept of society, comes into conflict with that which is living, and which, therefore, cannot be subjected to quantitative calculations. More precisely, it comes into conflict with those rights which, by nature, man exercises on his own and sole personal responsibility, that is to say, insofar as he is the author of new life, of which he is ever the principal custodian. . . .

. . . Consciences are today also afflicted by other oppressions. . . . Again, access to employment or to places of labor is made to depend upon registration in certain parties or organizations which trace their origin to the labor market. Such discriminations are indicative of a wrong concept of the proper function of labor unions and of their essential purpose, which is the protection of the interests of the wage earner within modern society, which has become more and more anonymous and collectivist.

In fact, is not the essential purpose of unions the affirmation in practice that man is the subject, and not the object of social relations? Is it not their purpose to protect the individual against the collective irresponsibility of anonymous owners? Is it not to represent the person of the worker against those who are inclined to consider him merely as a productive agent with a determined price value? How, therefore, can they consider it normal that the protection of the personal rights of the worker be more and more in the hands of an anonymous group, working through the agency of immense organizations which are of their very nature monopolies? The worker, thus wronged in the exercise of his personal rights, will surely find especially painful the oppression of his liberty and of his conscience, caught as he is in the wheels of a gigantic social machine.

Whoever would think that this solicitude of Ours for true liberty is without foundation when We speak, as We do, to that part of the world which is generally called the "free world" should consider that, even there, first of all real war and then the "cold war" have forcibly driven social relations in a direction which ultimately curtails the exercise of liberty itself, while, in another part of the world, this tendency has reached the ultimate consequences of its development.

APPENDIX E

PASTORAL LETTER

FROM THE ARCHBISHOP AND BISHOPS
OF THE PROVINCE OF GLASGOW
TO THE
CLERGY AND LAITY OF THE PROVINCE

ADVENT, 1955

DEARLY BELOVED CHILDREN
AND DEAR CHILDREN IN JESUS CHRIST,

Mindful of our duty as Pastors of the Flock of Christ to instruct our spiritual children in the way of salvation, and moved by the request of many of our working-people for guidance, we have decided to address to you this Pastoral Letter on a moral problem that faces us to-day.

It should by this time be obvious to all that the blessings of peace are immeasurably greater than any good that may result from war, however necessary and justified at times it may be to enter such a struggle. This is true in the industrial as it is in the international order. In industry at all times good relations between management and men are far more fruitful to all concerned and to the country as a whole than are disputes and strife.

Yet there are in our midst certain people who make it their profession and business to promote class-war and to stir up strikes in factories, regardless of the inevitable misery they cause in ever widening circles. Sheltering under the banner of justice and demanding the rights of the workers, in reality they have not the good of the workers at heart at all, but simply and solely the policy and spread of their godless and immoral organization, which, if it were to prevail, would bring in its train a reign of terror and a state of awful misery and slavery for all.

We do not hesitate to name these people. They are the Communist party, and their members, alas, are to be found in many places, democratically elected maybe, especially among the shop-stewards in our factories.

It is our solemn duty as Ministers of Christ and Pastors of His Flock to warn you against the evil machinations of these men who, under the pretence of seeking your welfare and vindicating your rights, are working relentlessly for your ruin. Prosperity in a factory they cannot abide, for they flourish most easily where there is discontent and unemployment. Indeed, they openly boast that bloody revolution, class-war and strikes are the chief weapons in their armoury. And they have added for our enlightenment that they are not bothered in their calculations with ethical or moral restraints.

Therefore they try to play upon the weakness of our fallen human nature, attempting to stir up the passions especially of greed and fear. They would persuade you individually, or organized in your unions, to assert claims that are unreasonable and therefore unjust and likely to ruin your livelihood; they would terrify you through their concerted action with the threat of unemployment by the withdrawal of your union card if you do not follow their lead or, at least, if you do not refuse to oppose their schemes.

To make our warning clearer and to give you, our beloved children in Christ, a yet more forceful lead in this matter, we now put before you for your guidance the principles that govern the justice of a strike and the so-called "closed-shop" or 100 per cent trade unionism.

FOR A STRIKE TO BE JUST:

1. Its cause must be just and not emanate from class-hatred or any other evil motive.

2. Its cause must be grave and not out of proportion to the misery the strike will create.
3. It must have a reasonable chance of success because of the seriousness of the issues at stake.
4. It must be the last resort, after all reasonable negotiating machinery has been operated and failed, so that all possible harm may be avoided or lessened.
5. It must not involve the breaking of a just contract, for it is immoral to break one's pledged word.
6. It must be carried on by just means, avoiding physical violence, intimidation and evil subterfuge.

THE CLOSED SHOP:

1. Always we should stand in the first place for the individual's right to work and for his freedom to labour where he will. Men are not born to be slaves.
2. This freedom is not absolute, but may have to be curtailed when the rights of others are threatened.
3. Therefore in some factory or group of factories, or even an industry, *when it is proved beyond reasonable doubt* that the general welfare and protection of the workers demand it, it would not be unlawful to institute the closed-shop.
4. With the strength of the trade union movement today and the general readiness of employers to co-operate with the trade unions, we believe that the need for the compulsory closed-shop is by no means universal.
5. Where the closed-shop is instituted, safeguards should be taken to ensure that the rights of the individual are not likely to be jeopardized or workers victimized by some pressure or power group among their fellow workers.
6. We believe in trade unions and would like to see all our people in industry and at work play an active part in them; *indeed we urge them to do so now more*

*than ever in order that these admirable institutions
may be always truly representative and democratic.*

We have been impelled to utter and issue these warnings
and statements of principles because of the threats spread-
ing even now to the welfare of several thousands of our
people. They are without wages and, likely enough, falling
into debt. Worse still is the wider menace that potential
sources of work may be lost to our country and moved
south of the Border, because of the conditions of industrial
unrest prevailing in our midst. Should this happen, the
dread evil of unemployment would undoubtedly result.

We hope and pray, therefore, that our guidance will be
heeded, that our people will refuse to be led astray by the
enemies of Christ and mankind, and that industrial peace
will be restored and remain with us for a long time to come.

"The Grace of Our Lord Jesus Christ, and the Charity
of God and the Communication of the Holy Ghost remain
with you." (2 Cor. xiii. 13.)

Given at Glasgow on the Feast of St. Andrew the
Apostle, Patron of Scotland, 30th November, 1955, and
appointed to be read at all Masses in all the Churches
of the Province of Glasgow on the Second Sunday of
Advent, 4th December, 1955.

✝ DONALD A. CAMPBELL,
Archbishop of Glasgow.
✝ JAMES D. SCANLAN,
Bishop of Motherwell.
✝ JAMES BLACK,
Bishop of Paisley.

APPENDIX F

EXCERPTS FROM THE CHRISTMAS MESSAGE OF HIS HOLINESS, POPE PIUS XII, DECEMBER 24, 1952.

THE CHURCH IS NOT LEAGUED WITH THE POWERFUL

42. Let no one think either that the Church, because she recalls these Christian principles, intends to protect an economic, or even a political system. Let us look at the facts. She has denounced and is denouncing the abuses of capitalism and the materialistic tendencies of the system issued from economic liberalism, because that system does not respect the dignity of the individual and because it has begotten a materialistic world in which man, and particularly the workingman, can only with difficulty live a life worthy of God and of himself. But the Church knows from experience as well as from the light of unchangeable principles, that a socialist or communist regime would not leave room for the exercise of lawful liberty, either to the worker or to anyone else; and, therefore, she has denounced and is denouncing all forms of socialism or communism. Because she is aware of the suffering caused by the dictatorship of capitalism, as well as by the dictatorship of the proletariat, the Church condemns the one and the other; and she denounces any political regime which is the accomplice of one class, or which tries to set up one social class against another. And in all this, she is concerned only in protecting the dignity of man. *The Church is the ally of nothing but the Truth and Charity of Christ.*

RELIGION, MORE POWERFUL THAN TECHNIQUE
AND ORGANIZATION

44. We are so accustomed to see the marvelous results of technical progress, and so plunged in an atmosphere of materialism, that we are too prone to put all our hopes on the strength of organization, and on the value of systems. Be on guard against such an attitude, dearly beloved brethren. If the industrial, commercial, and financial world puts all its confidence in the strength of its institutions and all-pervasive credit to maintain its present position; and if, in their search for a better world, the workers in their turn, in a spirit of reaction, rely solely upon the strength of numbers and abundant resources of their organizations, then eventually there will be a terrible and destructive smash-up, all the more terrible in as much as the opponents will be stronger, and all the more destructive in as much as the two parties will have used only their strength. The world which would result from such a smash-up would not be a better world for the workingman.

RELIGION, SOURCE OF COOPERATION

45. If, on the contrary, the work of restoration is accomplished in the light of the eternal principles of Justice and Charity, the parties concerned will ask of God and of religion a clear understanding of their respective functions in society and of the necessity of their cooperation for the common good, as well as the supernatural strength to fulfil their obligations. Instead of trying, either to maintain the status quo, or simply to overthrow the established order, they will work sincerely to keep what is good and to replace what is not worth keeping. And thus religion, as a result of its teaching on the nature of man, his family, his leisure, and his work, with the help of Grace, that indispensable factor in every good work, will become the basis of a Christian restoration of the workingman.

THE STRUCTURE OF ENTERPRISE

76. Evidently, these reforms must respect the nature of
the enterprise, and guarantee the legitimate rights of the
owners of the means of production. And so in his address
to the International Congress of Christian Employers, in
May 1949, after he had stated that the economy "is not of
its nature . . . a state institution", but "the living product
of the free initiative of individuals and of their freely
established associations", Pius XII declared: "It would be
just as untrue to assert that every particular business is of
its nature a society, with its relationships [between par-
ticipants] determined by the norms of distributive justice
. . . Such a conception stems from the assumption that
every business belongs naturally within the sphere of
public law. The assumption is inexact . . . The business
. . . falls within the competence of the private-law discipline of economic life . . . The owner of the means of
production, whoever he be — individual owner, worker's association or corporation — must always — within the limits
of public economic law — retain control of his economic decisions." (34)

77. Structural reforms, therefore, must preserve the
juridical private nature of enterprise, while seeking to
better the "other personal relationships [between par-
ticipants] which must be taken into account — even those
of shared responsibility." (35) Over his economic decisions, the owner will always continue to be master, if the
voice of the workers on the management committees of
the enterprise is only consultative, or, if deliberative, in
the minority. It is true that We have not to point out the
practical methods by which the participation of workers
in the life of the enterprise, can be brought about, but We
believe it to be our duty, dearly beloved brethren, to direct
social action towards a reform in this direction; a reform
which ought to be introduced step by step, with prudent

daring, and in a spirit of loyal and mutual confidence. Capital and Labour have everything to gain from it.

PROFESSIONAL ORGANIZATIONS

99. To fulfil the role which is theirs in the national economy, to promote their professional interests, to realize their legitimate economic and social claims, the workers ought to unite in solid professional organizations. The Church, since Leo XIII, of immortal memory, has proclaimed the *right* of the workers "to unite in associations for the promotion of their interests." (53)

100. Present circumstances render still more pressing and imperious the *obligation* of the workers, as also of the employers, to exercise that right. On this subject, let us recall, dearly beloved brethren, the doctrine of the Church. It is summed up in a letter written by the Sacred Congregation of the Council to His Excellency Msgr. Liénart, Bishop of Lille: "1 — The Church recognizes and affirms the right of employers and workers to form industrial associations, whether separately or together, and sees in them an efficacious means towards the solution of the social question. 2 — The Church, under existing circumstances, considers the formation of these industrial associations morally necessary. 3 — It is the desire of the Church that industrial organizations should be founded and conducted in accordance with the principles of Christian faith and morals. 4 — It is the desire of the Church that industrial associations organized by Catholics for Catholics, should be constituted among Catholics, while recognizing that special circumstances may necessitate another course." (54)

101. Every man has the duty to see that all his professional interests are protected and secure. He has the duty to aim at obtaining for himself and his family all that is necessary to lead a truly human life, sheltered against the chances of the future. He has the duty to co-operate for the welfare of his fellow-citizens, especially those to whom he

is united by common interests. He has the duty to collaborate for the restoration of a more balanced social order by favouring the respect of justice in all the activities of labour, industry and commerce. The isolated worker cannot achieve this. United with his fellow-workers, he will be able to perform that imperious social duty. In the present state of things, therefore, there is a moral obligation to take an active part in the professional organization.

102. It must be added that such an organization ought to draw its inspiration from the *social doctrine of the Church*. Leo XIII wrote in his encyclical *Graves de communi*: "That is the reason why We have never encouraged Catholics to form associations to better the lot of the working class, or introduce other schemes of the kind, without at the same time warning them that such things must not be attempted without the sanction of religion, without its inclusion and aid . . . For it is the opinion of some, which is caught up by the masses, that 'the social question,' as they call it, is merely 'economic.' The precise opposite is the truth, that it is first of all moral and religious, and for that reason its solution is to be expected mainly from the moral law and the pronouncements of religion." (55) And Pius XII said to the Belgian Movement of Christian Workers: "The Church gave them (to the trade-unions) her approbation, always on condition, however, that, based on the laws of Christ, as on an unshakeable foundation, they would work for the promotion of a Christian order among the workers." (56)

103. Consequently Catholics have the duty to support the professional organizations which choose as a guide for their action the social doctrine of the Church, and whose leaders admit moral authority in matters economic and social. The mass of the workers receive their education almost insensibly from the association to which they belong. The spirit, the vigour which pervades the organized unit proceeds from the mind and the heart of the leaders. That vigour reaches afterwards all the members and con-

veys to them a particular concept of social life and professional relations. Hence the association is formative. It will be such in a Christian way, if it expressly adheres, in its very constitutions, to the social principles of Christianity, and if the leaders who shape its action are capable, through their living faith in the authority of Christ and the Church, of submitting their conscience as leaders to those principles. Otherwise the association will lead the worker astray to materialism; it will imbue him with a false concept of life eventually made known by harsh claims, unjust methods, and the omission of the collaboration necessary to common good.

104. That is the reason why, dearly beloved brethren, on many occasions already, and particularly in our joint Letter of 1941 on *The Restoration of Social Order*, We have vigorously recommended the *Canadian and Catholic Confederation of Labour* (C. C. C. L.), and We have recalled the duty of every one, whatever be the social class he belongs to, to second and favour the unions affiliated to it. We now return again to that subject, insistingly asking the workers to join in greater number these unions, and urging all citizens to grant them a loyal preference and an entire support. Of course that Confederation, just as any human undertaking, is not perfect. But, given the sincere collaboration of all, it will better improve its technique of organization and representation, deepen its beneficial influence upon the working class, and, by its educative action, contribute to raise up the workers' moral, professional and cultural standards.

105. The *ends* that the labour unions must have in view are at once extensive and precise. These unions are not intended to set themselves against the employers or their associations. It is their duty to search for understanding and harmony between Capital and Labour. It would be a grave mistake to consider them "as a weapon exclusively designed for defensive or offensive war which provokes reactions and reprisals, as a flooding river which submerges

and separates"; when they should rather be "a bridge which unites." (57) The "trade unions arose as a spontaneous and necessary consequence of capitalism, established as an economic system"; (58) they came into being in a spirit of defense against the abuses of this system. We take pleasure, however, dearly beloved brethren, in noting that the Canadian Catholic unions, since their foundation, have expressed, in their Constitution, their will to collaborate and their desire that "peace and harmony exist between employers and employees." (59)

106. The pursuit of understanding and harmony between Capital and Labour is not a hindrance to trade-union action, but rather the indispensable condition of a prudent and courageous evolution, it will produce lasting and firm results.

107. The will to collaborate will not hinder therefore the labour unions from being loyal to the legitimate professional interests of their members. On the contrary it will help them to pursue more faithfully their immediate and direct aim, namely "furnish the best and most suitable means for attaining what is aimed at, that is to say, for helping each individual member to better his condition to the utmost in body, soul, and property." (60) In seeking these temporal advantages which do not constitute a supreme aim, one must strive for moral and religious improvement in order to exalt the dignity of the human person of the worker and to facilitate the pursuit of his eternal destiny.

SMOOTH RUNNING OF THE ENTERPRISE

126. Employers bear the primary responsibility for the economic life of their enterprise. Their right and duty is to ensure its material prosperity and its financial stability. An economically sound enterprise brings higher revenues to the owners and managers, and above all, it offers a valuable contribution to national economy. Conscientious em-

ployers rightly draw satisfaction and honour from successful results.

127. There is also a source of honour for the employer
in the smooth running of the enterprise for still another
reason. It allows him to render justice to all, and in particular to pay adequate wages, constantly to improve working
conditions in the shop, to guarantee regular work to as
many workmen as possible, and to offer his products at
prices which meet the consumers' convenience. Well aware
of his heavy responsibilities, the employer considers it an
urgent obligation for himself to avoid useless expenses and
to improve production methods. His profit, as a determining factor of prices, is limited by the rights of workmen
and the exigencies of common good. He knows that his
moral responsibility is involved in the quantity and quality
of goods turned out or of services rendered, in the nature
of publicity and in the determination of sales prices. All
deviations on any of those points sooner or later engender
a perturbation on the market and upset economic life to
a certain degree. The whole society is thereby affected, but
the worker's family, first of all and more heavily, bears the
repercussions.

NECESSITY OF EMPLOYERS' ASSOCIATIONS

134. It is not only a right but also a duty for the employers as for the employees to unite in professional
associations. By combining their efforts and activities the
employers will meet with economic, social, and moral advantages; they will thus find it easier to perfect their
technical knowledge and contribute to the bettering of
the laws on labour and economic life; they will obtain
a sounder idea of their rights and duties: they will investi-
gate together the social doctrine of the Church; their social
understanding will gain also through these associations.

137. The only employers' association to attain these
good results, dearly beloved brethren, is that which draws
its inspiration from the social doctrine of the Church. In

1931, Pius XI deplored the rarity of such associations. In our 1941 joint pastoral Letter on *The Restoration of Social Order,* We were obliged to make the same observation. We are aware of the progress made especially since then, in this sphere of social action. We hope for a redoubling of efforts in order to endow our region with an employers' organization, powerful indeed by the number but mostly by the quality of its members, firmly set on Christian social principles, full of respect for the particular needs of each professional group, and uniting in a Confederation the employers' federations of diverse professions. This employers' organization would be a step further toward the vocational group system.

138. The life of an employers' association follows the same rules as that of a union (nn. 113–115). It is imperative first that the employers, in spite of their many preoccupations, should devote themselves to the study of the social problem, having in mind at once the moral standards and the economic data. The time, devoted to the pondering of their social responsibility and to the research of means to meet it efficaciously, will bring them an enduring profit, all the more so since this study takes places in groups, adapted to the employers' needs, and functioning not only before but also after the founding of the association. Moreover, Catholic Action groups adapted to these milieux, if they received more encouragement, could helpfully contribute to increase the number of apostles among the employers.

139. Only under these conditions will there be developed employers' associations notable for the deep convictions and the Christian outlook of their members, and well fitted to serve them economically, within the limits of justice. The employers will become active members of their association in really participating in its life. One of their cares will be the correct choice of their leaders and officers, a choice which is, in an employers' movement, the more important because, the employer, occupied with

many matters, let their representatives enjoy a great liberty
of action. The latter, consequently, shape to their liking
the attitude of the association and give it a direction that
influences all the members.

THE EMPLOYERS' MISSION

142. If the employers are conscious of their rights and
faithful to their duties of justice and charity in the spheres
of activity just examined, they will be numbered among
the principal builders of social peace and harmonious understanding between Capital and Labour; they will thus
answer our appeal for collaboration toward the restoration
of the life of the worker. The Catholic employers' influence
on non-Catholic industrialists and employers is irreplace-
able. Armed with truth and moral strength, through their
membership in Catholic-inspired employers' associations,
they will be capable of introducing Christian social doctrine in the economic world, and of contributing substantially to the establishment at home of a social order in
conformity with the encyclicals, and therefore with the
very nature of man. Would not this social order be for
the other American countries, a living testimony in favour
of the value of Christianity? May the employers therefore
neither dread nor refuse the task that lies ahead! They will
not be alone in pursuing that end. Let them read from
time to time, together with the leaders of the workers,
the precious advice given by Pope Pius XII: "A great many
business men like yourselves, Catholics and non-Catholics
alike, have on repeated occasions expressly declared that
the social doctrine of the Church — and that doctrine alone
— is equipped to provide the essential elements for the solution of the social problem. Assuredly the reduction to practice and application of this doctrine cannot be the work
of a day. Its realization requires of all participants in the
process a discretion born of insight and foresight, a strong
dose of good sense and goodwill. It demands of them especially a radical reaction against the temptation to seek each

one's own advantage at the expense of the other partners —
whatever be the nature and form of their participation —
and to the detriment of the common welfare. It calls finally
for unselfishness of a sort which can only be instilled by
an authentic Christian virtue, sustained and aided by the
Grace of God." (81) To the bearers of Christian truth in
the world of economics, what a responsibility but also what
an honour for employers and employees!

RIGHT OF ASSOCIATION

174. The right of association is a fundamental one for
workers. It is given by nature itself. It is the duty of the
State to protect this right and to facilitate the exercise
thereof. No power may deny it to any group of workers
whatever, provided that, in a given association, nothing is
opposed to the common good and the security of the State.

175. It is the duty of public authority to shape a course
so that labour groups integrate themselves into the national
community and co-ordinate their activities with the other
elements of society in the service of the common good. It
should, however, apply itself to respect scrupulously the
very wise directives which were formulated by Leo XIII
in 1891: "The State should watch over these societies of
citizens banded together in accordance with their rights;
but it should not thrust itself into their peculiar concerns
and their organization; for things move and live by the
spirit inspiring them, and may be killed by the rough grasp
of a hand from without. In order that an association may
be carried on with unity of purpose and harmony of action,
its administration and government should be firm and
wise. All such societies, being free to exist, have the
further right to adopt such rules and organization as may
best conduce to the attainment of their respective objects."
(94)

176. The legislation on the right to organize, which has
already undergone happy modifications, should constantly
be improved so as to prevent the abuse by those who,

under one pretext or another, do not understand the necessity of sound unionism and the role for promoting order and social peace which it is called upon to play. If the workers cannot freely discuss with their employers collective labour agreements which protect all their legitimate interests, if they have not the legal means to parry bad faith in these negotiations, their freedom of association is an illusion. To narrow unduly the field of application of the collective agreements, to prevent even partially labour groups from exercising their representative function, would be an infringement upon their freedom of association.

177. Legislation concerning the right to organize should be elaborated in such a way as to guarantee to free and sound unions adequate representation in all the organizations which regulate economic and social activity; which would be a general extension of the excellent method employed in the commissions set up under the Apprenticeship Assistance Act. Moreover, freedom of association should be recognized in practice, thanks especially to the efficacious sanctions which the law would specify concerning dismissal or pressure exercised because of union activity. Finally, the executive power of the State must not interfere as such in problems of labour relations, except in case of grave necessity, to aid, for example, in re-establishing an equilibrium upset by the preponderance of those who exert too great an economic strength.

CONCILIATION AND ARBITRATION

178. Especially within an economic regime in which the vocational group system requested by the Sovereign Pontiffs does not exist, it must be expected that there will arise from time to time conflicts of interests between employers and employees. It is the duty of legislators to prevent these misunderstandings as much as possible, and to provide a useful mechanism of conciliation and arbitration to which the parties can have recourse with confi-

dence and with the assurance that their rights will be protected. However, in an imperfectly organized economy, it is practically impossible to avoid all conflict; lock-outs or strikes may occur. The moral principles which regulate the cases when it is permitted to use these extreme methods are well known.

179. There are certain categories of earners who would seriously endanger the common good by a concerted stoppage of work. In these cases, which however are not very numerous, the law may suppress or suspend the right to strike, but never without giving at the same time to all of these categories of earners adequate compensating means of obtaining justice; the law should, for example, provide arbitration with power of enforcement, possessing sufficient guarantees of impartiality, efficacy and despatch.

180. As strikes always bring about disastrous consequences and as they are justifiable only after the exhaustion of all normal means of arriving at a just understanding, the law may, for all earners, limit the exercise of the right to strike by imposing on those concerned the obligation to submit to certain procedures such as negotiation, conciliation and arbitration, before having recourse to stoppage of work.

181. The legal requirements relative to the prevention of strikes should always have in view and for effect the facilitation of an understanding between the parties in question and the maintenance of an equilibrium between them so as to induce them to continue the dialogue of negotiations. They should avoid even the appearance of partial or dilatory measures. On such delicate ground all incomplete or ineffective legislation which would not have the power to create among both workers and employers an atmosphere of legitimate confidence, but which would rather give them a feeling of frustration, would be prejudicial to public order because it would incite them to administer justice themselves and to scorn the law. In such instances the State should strive to correct and improve the

law. Leo XIII, in speaking of the evils of strikes and of remedies to apply, said with a great deal of wisdom: "The laws should forestall and prevent such troubles from arising; they should lend their influence and authority to the removal in good time of the causes which lead to conflicts between employers and employed." (95)

SUPERVISION AND APPLICATION OF THE LAW

182. It is very evident that all laws achieve good results only if they are applied with constant preoccupation for the common good and if they receive adequate supervision. Then they inspire confidence, facilitate obedience and cause authority to be respected. Conditions would be quite otherwise if partisan preoccupations or the desire to please financial interests should become the guide of public authorities in the supervision and application of the law. The best laws might be diverted from their purpose; their functioning would be misdirected. Inevitably there would arise among workers a distrust and indignation capable of engendering in their turn violence and contempt for authority.

SOCIAL EQUILIBRIUM

183. The common good requires, dearly beloved brethren, that between all social classes there should exist a sound equilibrium and a harmonious collaboration. In all legislative measures, as well as in their attitude, men in public life should be careful not to create opposition or suspicion between the different groups of society, but should seek rather to arouse good understanding by removing all the obstacles which are in its way. Like the Church, the State cannot be the ally or the accomplice of any class. Over all groups which it integrates and regulates, the State exercises its social authority, both superior and moderating. And as in the economic field it is the weakness of the workers which prevents maintenance of the equilibrium, it is rather to them that the State gives its sympathy.